Hive-Mind

Hive-Mind

a memoir

Gabrielle Myers

Lisa Hagan Books

Powered by ShadowTeams

Book Design: *Katherine Phelps and Kimberley Heurlin*
Cover Design: *Kimberley Heurlin*

ISBN: 9780976498698

DEDICATION

Hive-Mind is dedicated to the memory of Laura Trent. The world would be better with her in it.

Hive-Mind is also dedicated to Rose and Charles ("Snuffy"), my mom and dad. Thank you for giving me life and loving me for who I am. You've shown me that we can recreate ourselves and determine the stories we tell ourselves.

ADVANCED PRAISE FOR HIVE-MIND

"In powerful lyric prose that sometimes can't help but give way to poetry, in a book that simultaneously celebrates and mourns mothers, mother figures and mother Earth, Gabrielle Myers sings her own, very personal love song to the soil under all of our feet. The voice in *Hive-Mind* is complicated, edgy, vulnerable and deeply in love with fig trees, cherry tomatoes, and the sound of crickets on a hundred and ten degree summer day. In these dark, environmentally catastrophic times, we need books like this one to shake us out of our slumber, remind us where we came from, reconnect us to what we are."

–Pam Houston, author of *Contents May Have Shifted*

"It's gorgeous. The writing is so precise and riveting that you can't tear yourself away from any moment. Myers is a writer of elegance and heart, and also of extraordinary intelligence. I'm not quite sure how you create this hardhearted and yet spiritually elevated work; but she has somehow managed it. It's a remarkable experience to read this book. So please do."

–Wesley Gibson, author of *Personal Saviors*

Gabrielle Myers tells us, "I know I will come back to it, because now I learn we are similar, an implicit part of her I understand thickens like a roux over a high flame."
So, too, do I know I will return to this intimate examination of experience, which offers insightful, hard-earned revelation. As one reads this text, what begins implicitly, suggestively teased forth by Myers' deftly honed articulation of event, will be a strongly intensifying respect for how individuals come to understand each other, and how we come to understand some of the great challenges of our human condition, in all our unique particularity.

–Rusty Morrison, Senior Editor and Publisher, Omnidawn Publishing

"In a daring mix of poetry and prose, Gabrielle Myers explores desire and rot, walking close to the plum blossom's open mouth. I admire this book completely."

–Marilyn Abildskov, author of *The Men In My Country*

OTHER WORKS

"Woman" and "Pleasants Valley" appeared in the
Solitary Plover, Summer 2008

"Lament for My Sister at Harvest" was published
in *Damselfly Press*, Issue 4

"The First Rain of Fall" was published in *Fourteen
Hills*, Vol. 16, No.1, 2010

Contents

HIVE-MIND

California, February 2006: The Farm

I've spent three hours seeding tomato flats: Costoluto
Genovese, Cherokee Purple, Flame, Sungold, Green
Zebra, Black Cherry—the name for each variety more
interesting than the indistinguishable ridged seeds I plop
into each hole. Rain drips down the plastic sheeting of
the greenhouse. Before she enters, the rain beats so loud
all I can hear is water-needles hit plastic.

Then Laura's red-webbed blue eyes peek out from
her yellow rain jacket's hood. She almost topples over
as she lifts the foam rectangle that acts as a makeshift
greenhouse door; water drains from her jacket into the
dry soil of abandoned seed plugs.

"Looks like we've got a break in the rain coming. I was
thinking we could pull some weeds near the blackberry
vines before the next wave of storms starts up again—
you can just leave all these seed trays right where you
have them and come with me." She tries to look at me as
she speaks—maybe it's because we just met, but she can't
sustain eye contact for more than a few seconds without
turning her eyes to a corner rip in the greenhouse plastic

that lifts and falls when the wind blows in sweet mud smells from the upper field.

Underneath new-leaved vines, we bend, pull, and shift our legs further along the row. The yellow flowers of February oxalis jut from between old blackberry bark knotted in each turn toward the sun. After working ten-hour shifts on the line all week during my restaurant's annual "Whole Hog Dinners," my hamstrings and lower back tense and make each bend slightly painful. Laura works swift and quick; she maintains a lead of about five vines. When she speaks, she turns her head and lips in my direction so I can hear her, but her lean torso and muddy fingers face vine and weed.

We talk about local restaurants, the Hog Dinners, and a dish she had last summer at Chez Panisse: grilled squid with aioli, basil, and her farm's Sungold tomatoes. Our food talk leads into war talk and Bush talk. Over the two days that I've now known her, this conversation fluidity seems to happen in every exchange we have, but it's not just her; I find myself linking things that seem completely disparate in the space of two sentences.

HIVE-MIND

Last evening at dinner, over a salad of greens we harvested less than one hundred feet from Laura's makeshift mobile home, I talked about cooking and how I had dreams of owning my own restaurant with an acre in the back, and in the next sentence I was mentioning a photography exhibit I saw at the SFMOMA the week before. The two thoughts were related in my head, but when I tried to explain their connection to her, I fumbled and ended up exclaiming how different greens just clipped from the ground taste compared to their bagged and boxed restaurant versions.

From Bush talk, Laura slips into philosophical talk, which seem so entirely related, I don't have to stop and stretch my mind around anything.

"The last decade we've taken ourselves back about one thousand years—too much self-interest: we swim in ourselves." She pauses for a moment to tear free a particularly deep-rooted weed, then continues: "If we could give up our individual minds, cast ancient patterns of thought aside and join with our whole consciousness, with our whole mind which acts to benefit the many rather than just ourselves… well, that seems like the only way to get beyond where we are at now—to get beyond this wall we kept hitting our heads against…"

We pull and shift, each motion for Laura becomes a dance routine she's practiced, but my movements feel cumbersome; I get caught up pulling a creeping blade of crabgrass that inches toward the gnarled vine bark, only to pull up a five-inch carpet of green I meant to leave in the ground.

I'm not sure I buy into, or even understand how leaders can have much power over us; maybe growing up in D.C., surrounded by politicians and their children has always made their power seem deflated and finite to me.

"Do you watch Star Trek?" I ask, struggling to make a clean break with the too easily uprooted green patch.

I can't hear Laura's answer, so I just continue, "Remember the Borg episodes, how the Borg, or the big network or whatever it was, all worked in, or toward one consciousness… there was no me or you of any substance within the hive, except I guess the queen who controlled the direction of that consciousness… I don't think I could

4

ever live like that, but maybe something similar would be the way for us to go?"

"Yes! The Hive-Mind! In a hive, bees work to sustain the hive, not themselves. The drones mate with the queen, the workers gather pollen and water, and everything seems to work out better for their whole colony than it does for any group we humans form—or rather, can't ever seem to completely form."

"The Hive-Mind! I like that!" I want to say more to Laura, want to continue what feels like an important conversation—the Hive-Mind—but no thoughts come into my head except amazement that I'm here, on an organic farm in California with Laura, pulling weeds as the early spring sun seems to break behind a massive storm cloud. I'm going to move to this farm in less than two months.

I could never conceive of this possibility two years ago when I took a break from working the line at a winery restaurant back in Virginia. Each day tenuous, I sat on a rock looking out at a grapevine's green-pulse and the Shenandoah Mountains' dark-blue rise.

California, April 2006

Our feet sink into the mud as we cross the seasonal stream that divides our yurts from the fields. Over forty days of rain: now mud, mud, mud. Puddles form on the surface of the soil, reflect huge cumulous clouds, intermittent sunlight, and plum tree in blossom—their white petals fragile in the cool rains.

The yurts, one for Addie, the other intern, and one for me, are basically heavy canvas tents reinforced with wood, with wood floors, and wood burning stoves. Only a fifty-foot swath of verdant grass and stray plums trees separate our two yurts, but as Addie walks down the path, I feel like I am suddenly alone in this wild place with green oak leaves leaning over the yurt's flimsy roof. I have tea candles, a rechargeable lantern, cell phone, and an adapter to charge my computer while I drive—set for summer with no electricity and uncharted time to think and write.

This morning as I was still in a daze, we set up the chickens' new roaming grounds. My hands bruise from the wire and plastic ties, stain from the mud. Tomorrow we move the little ladies to new ground. In addition to chicken feed, as a treat Laura gives "the girls" aphids that have ambushed the tips of flowering kohlrabi and turnip greens.

We've taken to calling Laura "Farmer."

"Hey Farmer, where should we put these feeding canisters?"

"Hey Farmer, what made you want to become a farmer?"

Perhaps in retaliation, or just for fun, Farmer calls Addie "Baker." Farmer claims she needs to use this name for Addie because Addie doesn't look or act like an Addie. Addie explains she usually goes by her last name, Oliver. But Farmer has a cat named Oliver, and every time she says the name she thinks of her cat's bloated tummy, not Addie. Perhaps to make me feel included, Farmer begins to call me "Chef," which after a day becomes shortened affectionately to "Cheffy."

April, 2006

Some places take a journey to arrive at: face closed
doors and silent moments when nothing can be said and
you don't find anything interesting, not even yourself.
You have to get through nights when you couldn't arrive
at the resolution of a cricket call without drinking or
smoking yourself into oblivion. You have to get through
wondering how the hell you can remain upbeat and
sustain yourself when everything around you—from the
gas burning on the stove, to the dishwasher pinching
your arm, to the sixtieth mixed lettuce salad—yells wake
up to all these details you pass over daily. You know you
miss something that you shouldn't be missing.

Get through and here: you arrive with the air clear after
yesterday's storm and scented with expanding greenness,
plum and lilac blossom, but you cannot feel the growth
as you know you should, as something that comes from
inside you.

In the early evening, we went on a hike up an old
county road to a ridge top where we could see the
square swaths of Sacramento Valley farms, Sierra peaks,

Sacramento's black buildings, and the webbing of Delta marshes. Everywhere was green. In a pasture near a cow-bitten fig tree: lupine and chicory flowers.

We walked to a look out point and gazed at the farm from our hillside perch. The sun just set. Peeper frogs began their chant. The song rose from the valley up to us on the ridge; each frog's voice became a note, blurred into a rhythm that beckoned me. This place: life burst beyond any holding point.

When we got back from the hike, down in the lower field the first group of night stars came out. I stood in the middle of the onion and chest-high fava bean field, alone.

I thought of this line from a Mark Strand poem: "In a field/I am the absence of field./This is/ always the case./ Wherever I am/I am what is missing."

But I felt the opposite of those lines.

I am the presence of field.

We must continually fling ourselves out from prisons. Cast ourselves out from how we conceive of our existence; abandon the sick self. I don't know what fears are mine anymore. I don't know how my shape will rise up, a shadow behind me as I walk close to a plum

blossom's open mouth.

April, 2006

Farmer tills as the dew evaporates, finally able to get her tractor on the fields without compressing saturated soil and getting three large wheels stuck in mud. She rides back and forth all day under the spring sun's clarity. Farmer's Jack Russell, Lily, runs behind her tractor to catch mice scurrying from their holes.

While Farmer is very messy, she's oddly controlled and clear about how she wants us to plant seeds smack in the middle of each plug and harvest the hardneck garlic with a certain pitchfork. Things out of place on the farm include: Pellegrino bottles thrown at the corner of fields and beside the potting shed, cardboard boxes from last year left to rot on a walkway between rows of pea and fava greens, orange rinds left to decay on the driveway, stacks and fallen stacks of soil-filled seeding trays and flats near the two seasonal greenhouses. Tomato seedlings crowd the greenhouse tables. Weeds and small tags cover the gravel floor.

Farmer's friend, Jules, lives in a yurt about two hundred feet from Farmer's mobile home. I can tell where she's established her domain because the rocks on her path suddenly align; the steps leading into her yurt swept clean of grass and mud.

April, 2006

Baker and I are on greenhouse cleanup duty. We have a huge plastic bin filled with bleach-tinted water between us. We drag armfuls of the bent, sometimes cracked seeding trays and flats over to our station; chunks of soil and vermiculite fall to our mud-ringed boots.

Sometimes the soil cakes into each plug, and I use a broken plum branch to pop out the hard soil. Baker's large-rimmed glasses fog up a little from her soil-smudged fingers. Her red visor holds her brown hair against her ears. Every hour or so she pulls out an Marlboro, and holds it with her knuckles facing out like my boy cousins used to—I always thought this gesture made them look macho.

I am trying to figure out Baker. While my intentions for coming to the farm are clear to me—to take time away from the pressure of restaurant work; to take time away to write and redefine who I am to myself and what I am capable of—how she got here seems less obvious and predictable.

This is what Baker tells me as we poke and shake the

13

flats, little mounds of soil accumulating near our feet: she grew up in Brooklyn, and has been an urban dweller all her life, with stints in Boston and Manhattan; she dropped out of rabbinical school in her mid-twenties; she bakes for a living, but took a break when she moved out to San Francisco last October; before coming to the farm she worked in a secretarial position at a real estate office for six months; for three years she owned a bakery with her now ex-partner in Boston. They started a small bakery and cafe soon after they met—the neighborhood swooped to devour their seasonal pastries like blueberry upside-down cakes hot from the oven and glazed peach crostatas flaking with layers of butter. She would get up at three in the morning to begin baking, and her partner would work the afternoon shift. After two years of twelve-hour days stretched between them, they started fighting and Baker felt trapped. She left her partner, sold her half of the business; a few months later she came to California.

In just a few hours I feel like I've made a friend with Baker—she's the opposite of Farmer in that she speaks

14

at just the right time, reassuring the person she's talking with that their conversation is important. I've seen the way she does this caretaking with Farmer too, and with the neighbors, Janice and Steve, when they wander over to find their stray dog. Maybe it's Baker's religious training, or just who she is, but she seems like someone you can confide in—in turn, like someone who confides.

Once I get her to talk we are on a roll, but then she lapses into silence for long periods, like she's gestating, healing over something divisive. Each night Baker, Farmer, and I go to our separate quarters; while it seems like Baker and I need that solitude to get back to something, Farmer seems to want to get back to the solitude and stay there. Farmer mentioned Baker's younger stepsister died recently—a sudden aneurism. When I asked Baker if she had brothers or sisters, she only mentioned a brother and stepbrother. I guess I would edit too, considering that we just met.

Maybe it is better not to mention tragic stuff when you first meet someone—a rule I didn't follow after the incident with Mom—I needed to talk about the horrible thing, get it out of my mind by saying it in language, saying the words so someone else could digest it with me.

Last night I didn't have to use the wood stove to heat the yurt, and it hasn't rained for ten days. My third week on the farm, and spring's water has already begun to make its way into the plum trees. From where we sit dunking trays, the plum stems seem spongy with rain. Thousands of tiny buds begin to enlarge on the naked stems, and the army of plum trees stands like a brigade ready to fire blossoms if the sun keeps up its light.

California, 2004

Sometimes silence makes its way inside us: the rain drained over our old roof and through the gutters, only countered by my steps on the wooden floorboards. This was silence and I didn't like it.

January second—a month from turning twenty-nine. Four AM and the phone wouldn't stop ringing, like an annoying alarm that morphs into your dream before you realize the noise happens outside of your head. In my attic room, the lights of Oakland and Lake Merritt blurred as a rainstorm pounded against the windows. Jessie spoke matter-of-fact, and Dad spoke low and slow. I can't remember how they told me, only that Mom was in a coma and "We think she's done this to herself."

What I remember: I called the airlines. I was panicked and impatient, but after pleading my case, I got a flight out of Oakland in a few hours. I dressed, packed, made coffee in our communal kitchen. The rain stopped.

I packed and waited outside for the taxi. This waiting took so long, or at least I remember it taking so long, that it divides my life.

We all segment our lives into before and after, into little compartments of cause and effect; dividing points allow us resiliency from sterile moments in which nothing blooms. In this wait I stood on the corner of 7th and East 19th Street. The vague light of dawn became more pronounced, but still hesitated through the clouds. I could hear the approach and splash of cars on East 18th Street; their proximity made the quiet less terminal, but each approach raised my expectations for the taxi, which did not come and did not come.

Water drained from trees and smacked the jagged pavement. Houses were dark, and I envied the sleeping. As I started to pace on the corner, step over cigarette butts and dented cans of Miller Light, a band of color pulled from an office building down the street. Out of the beige building's entryway cluttered with torn fliers, a rainbow seemed to spurt like a fountain just starting to fill with water.

The taxi came and I couldn't tell him anything, just that I needed to go to Oakland International. I wanted to express my anger that it took him so long to arrive, but I was empty of words and could only look out the window at the passing streets and houses. Rainbows ascended like water from a sea cucumber, shot out in every direction from highway on ramps and a Grocery Outlet's plastic awning. How could this world present me with rainbows on a day when I was certain I would never see my mom alive again? I sensed that when I returned to this city, the place would look irrevocably foreign, as if I had never inhabited it.

April, 2006

Baker's yurt has no stove or running water. My yurt
has a two-burner propane stove and sink. I've told her
at least twice she can use the stove or sink anytime, but
as far as I can tell she's never used it. I don't know why,
but while I retreat to my yurt to cook lunch, drink more
coffee, and write, Baker cooks in the outdoor kitchen.
In the pack barn, Farmer has a refrigerator stuffed with
market trades such as ground beef, cheese, and milk, as
well as drawers filled with last year's dried plums and
figs. We each gather what we want from the refrigerator
and go off to eat and cook alone.

Baker fills a San Pellegrino bottle she found forgotten
beside a bent farm flat with filtered jug water from the
pack barn. She sautés ground beef and spring onions,
chops red oak lettuce as the wind from Mount Vaca spills
over the farm's acres. I imagine her quietly chopping,
placing the knife carefully at the side of her cutting
board, and stirring the beef in a heavy iron skillet with
one of the chipped wooden spoons Farmer bought at a
thrift store. She arranges the curls of lettuce on a thrift

store chipped plate, and scoops the beef and onion mixture into the center. As she sits at the uneven table, her plate sinks toward the latest issue of the *New Yorker* she's been reading. This afternoon, when we harvest the intractable new hardneck garlic bulbs from their tangle with one another, Baker will tell me about the story she read at lunch, and make me understand more about the story than if I had read it myself.

Maryland, 1983

Dad sorted and culled the uniform peas, plopped each deflated pebble into my bag, and told me to toss and rub each one to inoculate it. I shook a small lip-torn plastic bag. The bagged mix was the softest dirt I'd ever felt. I wanted to be a pea.

Everything: dead in the Maryland winter. Everything: last year's growth. Honeysuckle vines, dormant green, still clung to the tulip poplar. Poplar cups from last spring rotted in the drainage ditch; little torn propellers released and left to the run-off of suburban lawns.

Dad's hands and fingertips, worn from his constant tearing, shimmied in the rough clay soil. Over–broiled chicken and lima beans at the dinner table the night before, he told us of a young woman whose breast cancer had spread to her lymph nodes: fluid erupted from her neck during surgery. It was Saturday, and he didn't have to go back to the hospital for two more days.

He reached into the bag with his blood-tipped cuticles. Each pea, a gem he placed in the thawing bed we prepared the weekend before.

HIVE-MIND

I couldn't imagine anything coming out of that trough: it was March, and my pet crawfish Sammy still hid under a wooden plank on the other side of the creek.

April, 2006

Farmer kicks off her high yellow boots on the porch by the mobile home's sliding glass door. The boots stick out tall against the collection of fifteen or so muddy and worn shoes gathered near the entryway. As she opens the fingerprint and bug-streaked door, Lily runs ahead through the living and dining rooms to their bed that overflows with shirts and boxer shorts.

The Spanish tortilla that Farmer made last night sits upright on a wooden cutting board in the kitchen. She's so hungry she doesn't get a plate, cuts the tortilla with a sharp knife caked with remnants of last night's slice. She swallows a large piece in two bites, opens her refrigerator, pulls out a hunk of cheese, and begins to cut it into thick chunks on the cutting board. Yesterday's harvest of fava greens and spring onions clutters her counter; dirt still clings to a Torpedo onion's outer layer. She swiftly cuts the shoot's top off and trims tough skin away to reveal a fresh pull's purple shine.

May, 2006

We take today off and head for the Yuba River, about
two hours northeast of the farm in the Sierra foothills.
Farmer says she wants to show us her favorite place on
earth. We're in a holding phase on the farm anyway:
yesterday we finished transplanting the last tomatoes,
and two days ago we harvested the last batch of greens
and beets for market. As Baker turns off Highway 49 to a
single lane road shrouded in manzanita and oak, I open
the window and smell greenness expand in the air. The
barrier between the sun and my body dissipates.

For the last two years, I've worked nights and run in
the morning, trying to make the light enter me—so I can
feel some heat, connection, or driving pulse from outside
my body. Even after a fifteen mile run on a ridge top,
nothing gets inside me enough to make me turn out.
Sun blocked by my foggy mind. But each day here, some
blinder lifts from me.

Yesterday, I ate my fried eggs and sautéed pea greens
underneath a plum tree; blossoms loosened and fell into
high grasses near the seasonal creek; green leafed out

beside frail petals. I could feel an emergence turn within me as the blooms revolved in damp wind. A piece I have been trying to unearth which has eluded me these past years—a fragment hidden under layers, like a cardboard box discarded last year, now covered with leaf dust and twigs. This is my question: what can I do to hasten its unhinging, loosen it further until it leafs out like the plum tree I am watching?

When we get to the Yuba, we walk along a fire road for a half-mile surrounded by oaks and little tufts of Indian paintbrush, and then dip down to huge granite rocks and small nooks of beach that make the shore. The river flows high and clear from snowmelt. Mica pounded from granite makes water sparkle with flecks of refracted light. I sit on a bald rock, hang my feet into the cold water, read Rumi and Robert Creeley, and write a poem about this epiphany I am trying to have about collapsing boundaries. Across the river, next to the white sandy shore, a wild plum drops petals into the glinting rush of water. Why has it taken so long to arrive here, my distance from the sun evaporating?

Baker and Farmer have begun long discussions, with
Farmer bending near Baker, as if she can't hear Baker's
words. Farmer seems to walk with a wider stance this
week. On the drive in, she joked with Baker about her
cautious driving. I try not to notice, or rather, try not to
let them see that I notice, because it seems like they are
trying to be discreet. Maybe I'm a little jealous as well: I
can't make anything as romantic happen in my life. Last
night Farmer visited Baker in her yurt. She strummed
Baker's new acoustic guitar, tried to teach her "Mary had
a Little Lamb."

And then it was very quiet. The peeper frogs near the
creek started up; a small group of crickets between the
fields and our yurts began to bleat. In the middle of the
morning I woke up to coyotes attacking something; their
yelps echoed across the orchards of Pleasants Valley. The
chain around the compound's gate rattled, and Farmer
made her way across the lower field.

May, 2006

Okra leaves tent out from the knee-high plants, create dappled shadows on the weeds we're about to exterminate. Baker and I move methodically between six rows planted in Cajun Delight and Cow Horn okra. When we go to the farmers' markets we can't specify the variety of okra we're growing: The Company has patented the seeds and will arrest any farmer who harvests and attempts to sell these varieties.

We use my favorite tool on the farm so far: the wheel hoe. The wheel hoe has two wheels and a broad plate in front that sinks down into the soil and lifts weeds from their roots. This tool works great to knock out swathes of shallow weeds in between rows, but can't get close to okra stalks without tearing a leaf or flower. The wheel hoe offers me a chance to exercise my biceps and triceps—a workout I've missed since moving to the farm. Baker hates the wheel hoe workout, so she uses the traditional hoe shaped more like a rake and shimmies close to the plants I've missed.

Baker has kept her room in the city, and every weekend

she heads back in to socialize and date. She returns to the farm with numerous stories about her dominatrix housemate, Autumn, and Autumn's new girlfriend, who's married and visiting from Michigan with her husband. Over the last few weeks, Baker and I have been sent to attack the okra weeds as a team, while Farmer tears down an acre of plum trees and enlarges her tract of tillable land. We pull and lift amaranth and purslane too mature to harvest for the market, and Baker tells me about her romance with Wonder Girl.

Wonder Girl works at some nonprofit in San Francisco that connects kids to their environment. Baker and Wonder Girl have been dating for six weeks or so. On their first date, Wonder Girl made popcorn with garlic ramps Baker brought from the farm. A few weeks ago, Wonder Girl took Baker to her parent's farm on the outskirts of Watsonville. Wonder Girl said the former strawberry fields adjoining their property couldn't be planted anymore because of years gassing with methyl bromide. The farmers were trying to make the soil sterile from fungus and bugs; now it's not able to support even the plants they want to grow. Wonder Girl's mother has a brain tumor they think is linked to bromide gas drifting into their home from a neighboring field.

The last two times we've weeded together, Baker hasn't mentioned Wonder Girl, and I wonder if is because her and the Farmer are together and trying to keep their relationship discreet and to themselves.

I push the wheel hoe dangerously close to a stunted okra plant: "How is Wonder Girl? You still seeing her?"

Baker stops hoeing for a moment and looks at me, her brown eyes tinge red as she begins to cut the deep root of a mallow: "I saw her last week. And well, she said it was so great to see me, and she wanted to be honest with me because, well, she cares about me…"

Baker takes a final shove into the soil, lifts the steel edge of her hoe and a mallow's long thick taproot into the air, flings the massive plant into empty rows on our right, "and she's started seeing this other girl."

After I tell her she will find someone even more wonderful than Wonder Girl, and never mention the Farmer or even hint at it, we continue our push through each row, sprout by plant unearthing each invasive weed.

Six weeks ago the three of us worked our fingers into

the freshly tilled bed, dropped transplants of three leaves

and five spindly roots into the soil, and packed the

earth around each plug of okra. Now single half-opened

flowers with black-eyed centers hide under each tender

leaf's canopy.

May, 2006

Over one hundred degrees for three straight days.

Even at 8 p.m., I can't stay in the yurt. It's so hot, I can't breathe in there. I sweat until my tank top soaks, decide to write outside, and fight with the bugs that land on my computer monitor, attracted to the meager light. I'm under the black locust tree. The half-full moon has just crested Mount Vaca.

Here I am, but my focus is wrong. I should be writing about how yesterday I came into the outer kitchen after my lunch break, and saw tears in Baker's eyes as she ate egg salad.

May, 2006

Baker and I decided to make a ground lamb salad and
coffee on our lunch break, and now we lounge around
the outdoor kitchen, circle our feet above gravel, and
stare off into field and orchard. Everything around us
springs up, as if the sudden infusion of warmth and
sun has urged every flower, bud, or growing tip to raise
itself in reverence to the light. Jules stumbles out of her
yurt, pulls up her boxers with her left hand, and runs
her right hand through her short grey hair. As she nears
the kitchen, she lights a cigarette, takes a deep pull,
and exhales before sitting in a plastic patio chair in the
kitchen's dining area. Jules offers Baker a smoke, and
snaps out her steel zippo to light it for her.

I've talked with Jules once before, when I first came to
work on the farm for a day in February. The rainy season
was in full swing, so Farmer sent me to seed tomatoes in
the covered greenhouse. Either Farmer or Jules took pity
on my cold toil, and Jules delivered a steaming cup of
coffee just as I was starting to get bored and sleepy. Jules
and I didn't talk much that day: I gave a brief explanation

of who I was and why I was there; she told me to keep warm, and if I wanted another cup to just ask, she'd be in her yurt.

Jules' bloodshot eyes: the skin around her eyes deep set and puffy. Farmer has mentioned she drinks too much. From her shaking hands to her eyes, she seems like she's in a hard place.

"I had the weirdest dream last night. I dreamt that I was on an archeological dig, sweatin' my ass off and digging into the ground near a cave. After what seemed like eternal hours of dust and hot sun, I found a tablet covered with hieroglyphs, which was weird because tablets of paper do not last more than a few decades. We never find them on digs—clearly that paper was placed there recently. Then the dream suddenly switched—you know how that happens in dreams—I was at The End-Up dancing the rumba with a hot lady, the lights zeroing in on us as she leaned closer to me..." Immediately Jules has both Baker and me cracking up, and she relishes the attention, embellishes further "Then she took her clothes off, and, man did she have..." Jules gestures with both hands to her breasts, and cups them forward.

When Farmer hears us laughing, she comes over to the kitchen. She still has her sunglasses on, so I can't see her eyes as she listens to Jules.

I can tell Farmer and Jules have been friends for a while because Farmer doesn't even humor Jules. She faces us.

Her smile fights against her weak attempt to be serious, and a side grin inches out while she says: "Gather the hoe, two pairs of clippers, two five gallon buckets, and meet me in the lower field." Her large sunglasses reflect Jules' white hair, our kitchen's roof, blue sky, and a single blossoming plum branch.

Woman

To Lorine Niedecker

Well, she saw woman created

out of sea undulations.

She located the abyss.

Gave up fighting herself—

to an enclosure where she paid

for seeing the light through a window,

just seeing the light mind you!

Lived penned within.

Planted seeds that grew slanted toward the light.

Saw people on the walls.

Only water for meals.

Now she saw from the striated sky

a folded golden poppy kind of light.

She did grow poppies

you know.

May, 2006

One day as we weed torpedo onion seedlings, Baker
introduces the game of questions. We each have our
question for the day, to amuse ourselves as we weed and
weed for what seems like weeks. I come up with silly
things like: "Can you eat the root of a wild mallow? It
does look long and tender, and the root skin seems just as
tough as a parsnip."

But at night, under the yurt's plastic sunroof clouded
with sticks and leaves, in my futon cluttered with books
and crumpled sheets, I think of all the questions I can't
ask yet, except to myself: "How can we change ourselves
when we can't change the tape that runs in our heads?
How can we get back the belief in our own possibility?"

Farmer wants to know about politics. Before she pops
her question of the day, she lifts oversized sunglasses
from her eyes to her tangled brown sweat-raised
hair, and pauses to makes eye contact with Baker and
me: "When will the United States admit we are not a
democracy, but a closed system controlled by five huge
corporations that determine what we see on our grocery

shelves, grow in our fields, and broadcast on our TVs?"
When she asks her political questions, a part of me
admires her indignation: she's still optimistic enough to
think that something will change.

Baker's question for the day, as we hoe the pepper and
eggplant beds of amaranth and purslane: "Where do you
hold something and for how long?"

Tears mix with sweat and mud on her sun-darkened
face as she leans over young ridged leaves planted in
uneven rows. A Japanese eggplant near her boots has
grown a fruit too early, hung on to it too long as the fruit
spread out in two sections both thin and bent, now it rots
at both ends.

This has become my question all night because I can't
sleep and have run the charge out of my lantern and used
all my matches to light the propane stove for dinner:
What is the duration for holding? Hate, loss, sadness,
even desire—if you don't hold these feelings long enough
to learn from them, you screw yourself, render yourself
incapable of forward motion. The epicenter of pain will
fragment and divide.

Virginia, 2004

Was this the beginning?

Mom in intensive care. Asleep for 72 hours. Fragile. Her face tough and adamant with furrowed brows, the most breakable thing I ever saw. Look. Look at her mouth. Caked in blood. Her tongue swelled from her own teeth gone crazy during a seizure. Plugged in: a machine breathed for her. Plugged in: a pump ate for her.

Last time I saw her I almost hated her. Christmas vacation. We all stayed in a cabin near the Russian River. Fights all weekend: her and Dad; her and Jess; finally, her and me.

I couldn't be her ally anymore.

She was drunk on the lemon vodka we all drank, but she was gone from where we were. One night after she and I were in the hot tub, she walked across the hardwood floors to the freezer where we kept the vodka, and left a trail of water slipping from her toweled body before she landed on the chair. When I emerged from the hot tub, she looked at me like I'd just done the rudest thing, scolded me for leaking water over the floor and not cleaning up after myself.

When she awoke from the coma she remembered my name,

but then her eyes became unfocused, and she was gone. She pleaded with us: "I want to go home! Why won't you let me go home?"

Outside snowflakes ticked against the window, accumulated on the roof's gutters. I wanted to open the window, bring her face to feel a snowflake's sting.

May, 2006

On days that I work with Farmer, we both lapse into silence for most of the time. Sure, we talk a little at first, about what we are doing, about what we've had to eat for breakfast. We do have growing, cooking, and eating food in common. I tell her I've become fond of amaranth greens sautéed with garlic and mixed into my eggs. She tells me she's taken last year's zucchini, fried it in bacon fat and created a well for her eggs in the zucchini. When she dips her bread into the yoke, the golden nourishment stays inside the zucchini well, and doesn't run all over her plate.

And we have poetry. Poetry unites us on the days when there is nothing to say. Farmer suggests we each take a poem and memorize it:

"We should be able to stick to a poem a week, don't you think? The work goes faster and seems less interminable when you have something to think about. Every season but this one I've listened to books on my iPod. This year I might make it to August before I put the headphones on," she shouts over belly high Sungold tomato plants we're trellising to the third ring of metal stakes.

The next morning, our pants soak in dew as we pull grass from between the tomatillos. Farmer recites the first four lines of an Adrienne Rich poem. I can't believe she's chosen Rich, my favorite poet since I was a freshman in college, when I bought her collection *The Fact of a Doorframe* at a used bookstore in Massachusetts.

Farmer's started wearing a huge sunhat over her curly hair, and with her sunglasses, I can only make out her sun-red nose and oddly delicate neck. She stumbles over every third word, then blurts out the rest of each line, as if she's been studying the poem since we broke for dinner last night:

The thing that arrests me is
    how we are composed of molecules
    (he showed me the figure in the paving stones)
    arranged without our knowledge or consent.

I've decided to attempt Sylvia Plath's "Berck-Plage." I have a bad memory from all my years of excess, but can

manage the first couplet without stopping to pull a note
card out my pocket:

> This is the sea, then, this great abeyance.
> How the sun's poultice draws on my inflammation.
> Electrifyingly-colored sherbets, scooped from the freeze
> By pale girls, travel the air in scorched hands.

Farmer laughs when I shove the card into my pocket;
I can feel the stiff paper bend and rub against my thigh.
Lily leaps from row to row in pursuit of a baby bunny,
and I look out over columns of green, imagine I am
viewing the sea Plath describes. Minute by minute,
as we fling the weeds onto the wooden cart, all I can
concentrate on is the word "abeyance." I'm not sure what
its definition is, but to me it means stop. I hear three
syllables swing into each other, and the idea of the sea
as a great abeyance joins with a phrase from Kerouac
that's been stuck in my head for years: "the end of land
sadness."

When I first moved to California, the sheer cliffs and
brief beaches felt like a sudden stop. All my fleeing,

all my motion from the east coast landed me here, and this was it. The sea made me stop; there was nowhere to go. Even though I was obsessed with Kerouac at the time, I never felt sad that the land ended. I never felt an abeyance before those clear muckless waves, but a joy that I had ended here, while broad cargo ships and pelicans set themselves against the horizon.

May, 2006

Vacaville Public Library:

Abey•ance

Etymology: Anglo-French, from Old French abaer to expect, await, literally, to gape, from a- + baer to gape, yawn — more at BAY
Date: 1640
1 : a lapse in succession during which there is no person in whom a title is vested
2 : temporary inactivity : suspension
— abey•ant \-ənt\ adjective

California, October, 1999

Twenty-four years old. My first fall in California. Oakland, 6 PM on a Sunday night. My second night off from answering customer emails at Previewtravel.com. I was in the city the night before, dancing, smoking pot, drinking whiskey and beer with my new best friend, Sheila, at The Top. I tried meth for the first time, felt my heart loud in my lungs, slept with her roommate and ex-boyfriend of many years, Clyde. At 1 pm, when their neighbor started blasting drum and bass, the beat thumped through the wall as it shook the bed's wooden frame; I watched a stray strand of my long hair vibrate in the sun for 3 minutes before getting up. I threw up in the hall bathroom, but Sheila smoked me out and then I could begin my commute back to the East Bay. I stopped at Orphan Andy's for a grilled ham and cheese before catching MUNI to BART and walking a mile from Lake Merritt station toward the attic room I had just moved into.

I don't know how it happened. I don't know why I let myself talk to the guy on the street whose eyes bounced with a speeding or spinning mind's tick.

He looked at me like he knew me.

He asked my name, and then said, "Yeah, Gab, I met you a month or two ago. We partied with your friend Craig."

His curly hair stood up to the breeze on Park Street; his right high-top sneaker tapped the sidewalk as a cigarette butt rolled and a candy bar wrapper skittered toward the curb; his hands reached to shake my hand, then he hugged me under the red tinge of the Kragan Auto Parts Store's neon sign.

He said he had a van. We should get in his van. He had some whiskey in his hand, a big bottle of Jack. I was too hung over to be sober and the weed I'd smoked at Sheila's was starting to wear off. We got in his van and he asked where we should go, but then he ended up insisting we drive up the hill—he used to live around here and knew a place at the top of this hill where the cops never went.

I didn't have a friend named Craig. I didn't remember hanging out with him. Maybe he meant my old boyfriend, Chris, and just got the name wrong? Maybe I was high or drunk when we last met?

At the hill's crest we were surrounded by upper-middleclass homes, clipped yards edged with alyssum and flowering camellias. I don't know how it happened, or why I let him convince me that we should get in the back of his van. Was it that we were drinking, and if the cops saw us chugging a big bottle of Jack they would arrest us?

In the back of his van there was nothing but a knit beige blanket, the kind my grandmother or aunt had on the back of a couch in case we got cold. I don't know what he said, or why I suddenly got freaked after three shots.

Was it that we were drinking so fast, and even though I drank a good amount last night, I still had to be careful because I'd just started taking a new antidepressant? Was it that I might pass out? Was it that this guy could kill me if he wanted to, or rape me? No one knew I was with him; no one could see us in the back of his van.

By now I realized that I didn't know him; we had never met. Did he make up the story of us meeting? Did he think we had partied together before, or did he make this up so he could take me away? My mind filled with stories of women who had disappeared and days later their bodies were found in vacant fields filled with wild fennel, mutilated.

I insisted I get in the front passenger's seat. I felt his hands on my shoulders, but I was still strong from gardening in

the Virginia summer and pulled myself into the front cabin. I
opened the window, just in case.

"I need to get back to where you picked me up," I told him,
and stared at Lake Merritt's now distant edge. I glanced back to
make sure he didn't have a gun or a knife, but he hid the bottle
of Jack beneath the blankets and jumped into the driver's seat.

He dropped me off at the same corner he picked me up from.
The sun had just set beyond Lake Merritt and Downtown
Oakland, in between the Golden Gate Bridge; the light's fade
cast a red glow against the liquor store where I stopped for a
Sierra Nevada and some chips on my way home.

May, 2006

I pass Farmer in the onion field; she focuses on irrigation drip tape and discarded cardboard flats in her tractor's path.

This morning, she didn't speak as all three of us weeded garlic beds. Our bare feet sank into the mud's coolness. She worked almost in a panic, pulled and pulled at switch-grass patches as if they choked her, not the garlic.

She doesn't meet my eyes until I say, "Hey Farmer!" and break her from the trance of cardboard and drip tape. She isn't startled, as if she knows I approach, but isn't sure if she should acknowledge my presence.

Then there's so much space, not between us, but the valley of the farm lengthens. Her teeth: ivory white set against tan Lebanese and Irish skin, sun-bleached deer bones in a fall field. Puddles form on the surface of soil, reflect huge cumulous clouds, intermittent sunlight, and plum trees in blossom.

June, 2006

I start to unload the van's refrigerated back. Boxes of young Purplette and Walla Walla onions, fresh Spanish Roja garlic, and various greens scent the old mobile refrigerator's damp air. My hands still stink, bear stains of onionskin and soil that we peeled or washed away from the bulbs hours earlier. I hear Stacy behind me, as I lift the thankfully light box of delicate fava greens. Stacy interned on the farm a few years ago; now she lives in San Francisco and works the Oakland and Berkeley markets with us.

"What are you doing?" She holds a grey fisherman sun hat in her left hand so I can see indentations of confusion on her forehead.

"Unloading the van…" I trail off—this isn't the answer she's looking for.

"We always take out the tent first, then the tables. Why don't you take a break, get some coffee? It's going to be a long day for you." I hop down; my ankles crack on impact with asphalt, and I let Stacy climb up into the van's dark refrigerator.

With coffee in my hand, I am happy. I've been up
since 5:30 AM picking pea shoots, fava greens, sweet pea
flowers, and pulling onion sets from the unforgiving
cement-like clay soil. According to Farmer, I won't arrive
back at the farm until eight or nine tonight. A long day,
but this morning I saw little white moths flutter over the
broad leaves of young summer squash; in the morning
light, thick ridges of leaves and thin purple veins of moth
wings webbed like routes on a map. In the field, we stood
among things we could eat.

Stacy takes a break to buy a raw vegan roll of seaweed,
cucumber, micro greens, and cayenne-cashew sauce from
the *Totally Raw* stand at the southern end of the market.
While she's gone, a woman I sold sweet peas to at Lake
Merritt Market comes to our stand and leafs through the
pea greens, ignoring the tongs set clipped to the edge
of the basket. She's sunk, as if she's looking up at her
motion through a foot of murky water. Her body curves
toward our undulating yellow tablecloth and billowing
plastic bags; her straight grey hair hemmed in by a large
purple garden hat. The previous week we talked about

the rain and the late tomato crop. She's planted her Sungold and Early Girl tomatoes in raised beds, but isn't sure if they will yield because of the incessant rain and cool weather this year.

I've spent too much time with myself the last month. Now I feel a blossoming need to talk to people. Any tidbit from their life, any connection, no matter how brief, will nourish me in the hours we spend pulling grasses from the base of onion sets.

When I ask her if she'd like to try the Egyptian Spinach, she hesitates, stops her shuffle of the pea greens.

"Oh, no. I can't eat greens like spinach. Must be the oxalic acid...keeps me up all night..." She cups her small belly with both hands; her eyes widen in agitation, "As I learned last night, after I ate lasagna that must've had some spinach slipped in."

I can't figure out a response. Egyptian spinach isn't really spinach, and doesn't contain oxalic acid. We just call it spinach so people won't think it's strange, so they can imagine mixing it into rice or pasta.

"Sorry to hear that... We do have some incredible pea

greens—just harvested them three hours ago! Here, try some." I gesture to the basket filled with curled pea vines.

"Oh. No thanks. Not today."

A man with a strained red face comes to her. The skin around his eyes loose and flush, his eyes ruddy with drink and sun. He wears an Oakland Raiders cap and white knee-high socks; his right sock slips down his calf. He guides her away by taking a tentative hand. They don't smile as they touch. She walks with hesitation; as she's led onto the crowded path, she looks back at our stand.

I spin scenario after scenario around her inset eyes, slouched frame, fragile tomato seedlings, and her man with the ruddy face. I want to know why she's reluctant. Why didn't she smile when they met? Why was she up all night? What did her lasagna taste like?

The woman isn't happy. That's all I know. The weirdest thing happens inside me as I realize it wasn't the spinach in the lasagna that kept her up last night. This woman is sick in some way, and spinach has nothing to do with her insomnia. I can't pay attention to the amount of change I give customers—I just start guessing. Maybe she's dying of something. What do I care about change and vegetables anyway?

I want to say something to her before she vanishes in the crowd of people and plastic bags, slow her departure, tell her that she can be honest, she can talk about the horrible thing. But I can't make the words move from thought into my mouth: they hover in my chest, in the inhalation.

The words hesitate, make my cheeks flush with anticipation until the situation where I can speak fades. These words follow the path that most important words have over these last two years; they stay with me until they cannot be heard.

I try to make change for twenties and unload boxes of pea greens, which sell like funnel cakes at a Renaissance fair. Earlier that day, I worked at a fast pace snipping sweet pea stems and pretended, putting away thoughts of mom's attempt to kill herself.

Why I can't speak about my mom to Farmer and

Baker, as they try to draw me into conversations on the greatness of Rocky Balboa?

Why do we avoid talking about the awful stuff, for fear that sadness might swallow us? Is life shitty enough without talking about the why and how of our shit?

I want to know how to hold what I saw two years ago in the hospital; how my mom became a mean stranger as she fought with the nurses in intensive care, didn't recognize my sister or me. How long will it be before I can stop acknowledging pain's ability to linger as I move down rows of spring greens?

I want to know what Farmer kept hard inside yesterday, as I passed her in the field on my way to the wash barn.

June, 2006

Is this the beginning?

Because this is the scene I will come back to, that I know I will come back to as I live it, as we plant the last batch of okra, as the sun sets spring glow over Mt. Vaca, as Lily runs into patches of wild grass hunting gophers, as Farmer, dusty brown in her dirty white t-shirt, gathers the plastic flats and places them in the back of her pickup truck. I know I will come back to it, because now I learn we are similar, an implicit part of her I understand thickens like a roux over a high flame. The idea of our similarity, and our essential difference, will scare and simultaneously make me thankful as I sit in my yurt that night typing a sentimental poem about the exchange.

I am still afraid of myself, of my potential to drink whiskey and beer night after night, even when it makes me sad and stuck; even when I've seen my mom brought down to the ground by wine and port and vodka; even when I've heard for years of my Grandpa's fall to Four Roses Whiskey and cigarettes. In fear I run marathons. In fear I've given up drinking for a year, stopped smoking pot from morning until night, and quit cigarettes. I've become sober out of fear of what I will become in my forties, of that black cloud that I feel begin as a seed in the back of my mind after a night of excess—how I feel this seed's incipient blooming, its wish to extend, to push beyond the barriers of my brain and edge itself into my heart, into my legs.

I don't understand how we begin our talk, or even the dialogue that builds up to Farmer telling me she struggles with giving up weed, how she uses it as I used it—to help her function like a normal person appears to function. We both hold the belief that we're chemically abnormal, that we have to smoke something, take something, work our asses off in a field, or run up one thousand foot mountains to attain the level of ease that others have toward themselves.

She tells me she's just started on an anti-depressant called Paxel. I tell her that stuff never worked for me; that I was on about four different anti-depressant and anti-anxiety meds from age eighteen to twenty seven—they just made more depressed and anxious. The only thing that worked for me was exercise, training my mind to stop and try to remember it's located in a body.

After I tell her about my mother's suicide attempt, she tells me the circumstances surrounding her mother's drowning accident: she believes her mother willfully took her mask off as she dove in the sea near the Channel Islands. But what confuses me is how Farmer tells me this—she says it with a sense of romance, longing, and idealization—her eyes don't focus on anything, but look away at the field's edge. Dragonflies zip around us and behind her; a large wing momentarily catches sunlight and spins it toward me.

I tell her I've discovered that I have this energy, and if I don't direct it at something positive, it unknowingly gets directed toward the negative. I have to harness the seed that could unfurl a black or green leaf —I have to tackle that seed and cultivate it.

"It helps to hear how someone else is doing it," she says.

I'm not sure what I'm doing.

Her eyes, blue like the sea's abeyance, blue like a

camera's full closure on an ocean's wave, how the white parts expand red when she tells me, in some words I can't catch, how she struggles. Sunset like a Moro blood orange peel. Contrast with plum-purple mountains. Green okra transplants look stupid and stoic on their first night in the field. Her hands, like mine, cake with soil. Our nails clot with dirt, baptized in loamy grains.

These words catch: "Sometimes I feel like a horrible person. I just want it to stop."

She sounds like she's sinking into the soil, folded in by the same grains that nourish okra. I hear the voices I've just silenced in my own head.

Were these the words my mother listened to as her mind reeled off all the reasons why death was a more reasonable choice than life?

We stop talking when we collect the flats on the back of her pickup truck, when the okra's watered in by the irrigation, when only one or two stars illuminate the moonless sky. Before she says goodnight and heads back through the rows to her house, she stands before her truck, her spine straightens, and she tells me to make sure I leave the farm tomorrow at 5:30 AM; if I leave five

minutes later, I might not be able to park the van and will

have to unload several blocks away from the market.

"And don't forget to pack the torpedo onions in the

wash barn and take a new tablecloth, the old one's

stained with crushed fava leaves."

June, 2006

I am always here, at the precipice, and so is this part—a shadow-self follows me down each trail and interaction.

This must be what she felt building for years.

What feeling drove her?

Was this shadow-self why she turned away?

Virginia, 2004

Two and a half years before coming to Farmer's farm:
Red Bantams, Anconas, Rhode Island Reds, and Plymouth
Rocks sauntered and pecked at the mud-exposed hill. From
this patch I harnessed tomato vines and plucked peppers, but
nothing of the former garden remained. Ramps and exposed
chicken wire littered the acre. I watched for discarded shovels
and pliers.

Jess and I drove cross-country along Route 10, past
Arizonian saguaro, New Mexican sagebrush, Texan oaks,
and the stunted cones of Virginian junipers. Mom went into
recovery in Williamsburg, and I went back to Virginia to stay
on the farm with Dad. I couldn't sleep at night, images and
words haunted me: Mom's mouth caked in blood, her tongue
swollen, the doctor telling us she might never be "who she
was." But I couldn't figure out who she was; she had changed
so much in the five years of heavy drinking, all I could count on
was that she would direct me whenever she could and hug me
whenever she could.

After decades as a type-A physical therapist and curriculum
developer, she started to sneak huge jugs of vodka in the garage

and take back pain meds to numb herself. Mom stashed her Smirnoff among old aquariums packed with dusty pebbles and worn tennis shoes.

And she raised chickens. Hundreds of chickens.

Chickens dominated the farm: roosters announced day; small chicks ran loose through the rusty clay; countless red and yellow bodies with scaled feet climbed in the mobile trailers that she hauled around the upper acre. Guinea hens skipped and scurried over the horse fence and hid in pine trees as she tried to gather them before nightfall. On a visit last Christmas, Mom and I spent a half-hour chasing the frenzied birds from the tool shed back over the fence until we herded them into the coop. Mom had an open dialogue with the chickens: she said hello to them by name, pleaded with Sammy, Matthew, and Billy to go home.

Hours she worked in the cold wind tying twine, erecting cages, and repairing fences to protect her chickens. It all went to waste. Dad had to sell the chickens and their shacks to pay for Mom's rehab. After passing through San Diego, Las Cruces, San Antonio, Gulf Shores, and Chattanooga, places we talked about wanting to just stop in to prolong our trip,

Jess and I stood before the chicken houses shoved together like a dilapidated mobile home park.

June, 2006

This is my question as I stumble out of the yurt in the middle of the night to pee near a baby oak tree: "Even if she tries to take a different path, is a daughter bound to mimic her mother?"

I say "No," not to myself, but loud, so that the peeper frogs and crickets can hear me and hold me to what I've said. I firmly pull my shorts up, and walk ten feet back to the yurt; my shadow thickens as the moonlight clarifies rock, stick, and acorn.

But lying on the futon I can't sleep. Filtered through the narrow sunroof and side panels, as if to dispute both my question and answer, moonlight strikes the rechargeable lantern, the bunk bed built for a surplus of farm workers, and wood floors dusty with dried mud. Steady cricket calls stop and wind picks through each stiff oak leaf. The stream once cascading with water barley trickles. Each object in the yurt seems illuminated for a reason, inscribed with a meaning I cannot decipher. Even the plastic water jug in the corner glows blue; through its plastic, I can see the water surface vibrate as the wind fingers the yurt's belly.

June, 2006

Farmer sleeps out under the full moon, guards the chicken coop against the animal that's been killing the "ladies." Death-count three. She found a chicken this morning, its head and upper body eaten, feathers strewn over grass in the run, rest of its body left to waste in early morning dew. Farmer has a shotgun, foam mattress, headlamp, and Lily by her side.

The moon rises up over the fields and humpbacked green hills.

As we snip pea greens from their stems, Farmer talks about stars, the moon, a coming meteor shower, and how without a tent there is nothing between you. That's how she says it, nothing between you, and gestures with her right hand into the air above pea vines thick with flies and moths.

She moves her foam mattress around the farm, from outside the chicken coop, to the edge of the orchard bee boxes, to behind her garbage cans and orange poppies.

I've been sleeping outside the last few nights too, two hundred feet down the slope from Farmer, with just a sleeping bag.

I'm under my laundry line filled with socks and dirt stained jeans—right outside my yurt, with a broom in case a raccoon or coyote tries to have its way with me.

June, 2006

When we break for lunch or dinner, usually we each go our own way—we meet back after an hour for work, or early the next day, and discuss our various successes with the farm's produce. Farmer seems excited to have a Baker and Chef on the farm, and we all have enormous appetites from the work. Occasionally, we take coffee breaks together, plan elaborate fish fries and hamburger dinners with every ingredient made from scratch, sourced on the farm or from our trades with purveyors at the markets.

Last year, Farmer built an outdoor kitchen with propane burners, makeshift marble counters from Urban Ore, a wood table, and gravel floor. No longer am I trapped behind restaurant walls and stainless steel; I can cook where food grows. I'll sauté onions and a monarch will float by, touch the wood table with worn sides, tap the black shade net above my head, and smell a lavender flower before careening out into the fields. If I need to throw in rosemary, sage, tarragon, parsley, or oregano, all I have to do is walk ten feet to the herb bed, and pluck away. Tough leaves of oregano, still fuzzy in their protective coat from winter, need to be held close to the board as I slice through a stack of herbs for our hamburgers' onion marmalade.

Farmer pulls out a can of San Marzano tomato sauce she made last season, and I acidify this base with locally made red wine vinegar we trade for at market. Farmer has an arsenal of food products produced from other market purveyors. Honey, crystallized and hard to extract from the bottle, eventually melts into my ketchup. I salt-bind the Prather Ranch ground beef we exchanged for early summer squash and onions. Last Saturday at the market, a rancher named Mike told me about his cow pastures out in the valley between Red Bluff and Lassen, and in the market bustle I imagined stacks of volcanic rocks and grasses so dry their grains pop in the heat.

Baker rolls our buns: each round of dough smooth and glossy from her kneading on the outdoor kitchen's butcher block cutting board. In Farmer's small kitchen, an old Wedgewood bakes unevenly; Baker has to turn the tray every few minutes to ensure all the buns brown.

Finally we sit down to eat; we're so hungry no one talks but Lily as she tries to jump on each of our laps, whimpering for a bite of our burgers. My burger's stuffed with caramelized onions, tangy ketchup, smoky crisp bacon, and creamy Cambozola spread over all the other ingredients. I've never been as hungry as I am on the farm: each day I think for hours of what I will eat or cook next; even parsley, usually so common and mundane, tastes more pronounced and sweet, green and minerally, like a mouthful of delicate grass pinched near a clear stream.

Farmer has a little two-quart ice cream maker, and Baker crafts Persian mint ice cream from mint that grows around Farmer's motor home. For our fish fry extravaganza Baker made salted caramel ice cream, so thick and rich that I snuck several spoonfuls into my coffee for three days.

After our quiet meal, we are in a food coma, and as our eyes glaze over, Farmer positions herself on the gravel floor. Her sunglasses still hide her eyes; her curly mass of hair rests against a pile of rocks littered with stray plum blossoms. Farmer's thick hands curl against her side; each wrinkle extends and fissures next to her pink sun shirt.

Baker follows her a minute later, and they both lay like sunning sea lions on our gravel kitchen beach. The sun angles itself across their faces—each freckle visible as their hands inch closer. Before they touch, I fall to the gravel, tired and full, not sure what else to do. My eyes close, but the sun hits my lids and penetrates.

Each morsel of light strikes some mirror in my brain, and all the summers I use to run for hours under the light and the Maryland creek where my sister and I would build moss bridges, come back. I will never be complete. A sort of piecemeal amnesia will render me incapable of simultaneously feeling all the ecstatic and horrible moments. All these moments I live will pass, I will forget, only for them to rise again, and change me when the sun gets inside the right way.

When I wake up, Farmer, Baker, and Lily are gone, and the sun has begun to lower, create long points of shadows from each plum branch. On my way to the yurt,

I step over a dead mouse Lily has slaughtered: its tiny
body split, liver smeared with grass. Hornets have begun
to harvest parts of mouse flesh.

June, 2006

This evening as I run, the sun has just set over Mount Vaca, and my ability to see gravel on the roadside lessens. My legs turn against the asphalt as I plod under branches of a live oak. I feel hot pockets of air, coolness near the creek creep from between fig and buckthorn trees. In this dense dry heat, the temperature change in the air hits more acutely; as night falls each degree drop registers to less sweat on my skin. Air fills with small flying bugs, wind picks up, rustles leaves as I run underneath a broad arc of canopy. A quarter moon and three stars emerge.

June, 2006

Over the last month a solitary wild turkey has roamed around the yurts and seasonal creek. Her large body and head bobs as it gobbles around drying grasses and valley oak seedlings. The light is clear each morning, evaporates the dew thick on leaves and grass seed heads.

Maryland, 1985

Mid-spring weekends Mom, Dad, Jess, and I raked cart after cart of oak, sycamore, and tulip poplar leaves under a blue plastic tarp and hauled them to the street. What most families did in the fall, we did in the spring. I thought we tried to take away the dull reminders of fall and winter, intent on displaying the azalea and red bud in all their glory. But the truth is we never had enough time: both my parents worked full time, commuted, and finished up lab reports or conference calls from their desks at home. Maybe we all got restless when the delicate fingers of green tents began to expand.

While each workday ended with a power struggle between my parents over how to discard the extra leaves, or how to trim the monstrous azaleas, I couldn't wait for these spring cleanup days. After an hour of work in the damp thaw warmth, my own blood extended, began to reach its full force in every capillary. A part of myself shut down by the winter's sleet, dark hours, and leafless landscape suddenly filled, urgent. The smell of half-decomposed leaves made me want to work all day among the still incipient redbuds. Eventually Mom and Dad left to prepare a spaghetti dinner, and Jess and I lingered by the broad stone steps in the backyard. We caught potato bugs and turned them over, watched their tiny legs attempt to grip our stick. We tore moss off old bricks near the cellar, and made pillows from the fuzzy verdant strips. Jess got bored, and went in to help Mom and Dad cook, but I stayed out until sunset, cleared leaf-mats away from the tender bases of tulips yet to flower.

June, 2006

Each morning when I wake up in the yurt, first I boil
water for my French press, and then make oatmeal
from the huge five-gallon container Farmer picked up
at Rainbow Grocery. I've taken to crumbling in walnuts
that Farmer and the winter intern, Lucinda, collected last
year from roadside trees. As the oatmeal cools, I force my
feet into my boots without bothering to tie or untie the
shoelaces, and trudge fifty feet to the composting toilet in
the outhouse. With fiberglass behind and to the side and
only a mesh net in front, I can see the bathing area and a
plum tree from my perch. Now with morning temps in
the mid-sixties, I've taken to sitting and relaxing on the
toilet every morning with my coffee. As I sit on the toilet,
I look out through a hole in the fiberglass and see a little
green plum pushing out from a blossom point.

No matter how I try to time it, Baker and Farmer
always beat me to our meeting place in the packing shed.
I don't think I'm late—at least according to my cell phone
I'm not late—so I assume they're just early. Even after
two months on the farm, I'm still not into this bright-eyed

in the morning/getting up at dawn thing.

At first, the Farmer would hastily be stacking boxes in the refrigerated van, or pulling the harvest cart behind her, with Baker following five feet behind, munching on bread. The last few weeks, on the days when one of us hasn't left before dawn to make the farmers' markets, they sit side-by-side on milk crates or lean against the harvest cart, laugh and smile. While a part of me is jealous, since I seem to be perpetually single and strike out with every person I care for, another part of me can see their love edging itself out from inside, and this could be the swing that Farmer needs to change her mind about herself.

June, 2006

Tonight I think about rodent skulls and bones in owl shit; how things I never thought of before now occupy my mind in bizarre little images—concrete gifts for my abstractions.

The three of us went across the street for dinner at the neighbor's house. As we ascended the gravel road, clusters of exotic cacti and spikes of white and purple flowers seemed to climb and compete on the driveway's sides. Squirrels scurried into bushes that gathered behind cultivated flowers. Towering Tuscan pines surrounded a house that looked designed by Frank Lloyd Wright, with large windows and dark clean wood angles. Marj and Steve invited us in, and we each grabbed a drink from tall thin glasses.

Since I arrived on the farm, I've drunk out of Mason jars or old coffee mugs Farmer picked up at Goodwill, so as I held an elegant wine glass and drank ice-cold lemonade, I felt like I was in a movie or a novel set in Italy. Something about the evening reminded me of a Forrester novel, maybe it was the intellectual banter between Steve, the prison psychologist; Baker, the former rabbinical student; Farmer, the law school drop out turned revolutionary cultivator; Steve's new wife Marj, the junior high school teacher; and Steve's ex-wife Allegra, the former ballet dancer and current poet. Even tonight in bed, I cannot remember the particulars of our conversation, except that we talked about everything—the war, the president, America, farming, housing developments in the upper part of Bucktown Lane, the local school system, the three dogs that snatched new potatoes and pork scrapes from under our feet and barked behind the gate as we approached and left the house.

Tonight, all I can think of is owl shit at the base of pines that Farmer showed Baker and me when we arrived at the top of the driveway.

The Tuscan pines point higher than anything else in the valley. From the turn before the farm and Steve's house, you can see the characteristic green spikes, as if you're approaching some countryside Italian villa. Some of the old fruit farmers in Pleasant Valley were Italian immigrants; their trances remain in the plants that live here: Tuscan pines, wild fennel, and the pistachio tree two farms over.

Right after we had drinks in our hands, Farmer took us to the pines, and picked up compacted cylinders that nestled on top of the trees' surface roots. The dry cylinders broke apart like sod, and tiny bones and skulls revealed themselves in the remaining dust on Farmer's tough hand. She dared Baker and me to guess what it was, and knew of course that we wouldn't have a clue.

"It's owl shit!" She laughed, and pointed to the top of the pine tree. All I saw was the thin tip of new green flailing in a temperate wind. "An owl lives in the top of the tree, and these are the little mice she eats!" Farmer rolled a miniature skull between her thumb and index finger, displayed the pearl like a chef admiring a fresh white truffle.

"But how can it digest all the bones?" I asked, still not convinced that this wasn't something else, but inclined to believe Farmer since she would know something like this.

"I guess it just digests differently than we do," Baker
said, leaning to touch the fecal-covered bones with her
finger, her glasses inched closer to her nose.

Tonight, instead of thinking about the crickets as a
single loud drum, I think of the small skull Farmer held
between her fingers, and how she smiled, like a young
boy who's just discovered something magical and
potentially dangerous in the grass beneath his feet.

July, 2006

This afternoon Baker is at the Berkeley Market, and
Farmer and I work side-by-side as we tie tomatoes in
the lower field to the next level on their metal posts,
transplant a second round of basil, and set irrigation
pipes over transplants. Each task on the farm has its
dance: tying tomatoes requires us to let slip heavy string
at just the right pace, bend and swing the string under
each plant. I keep messing up the sequence of these
steps, and have to go back every five plants to restring
and tighten my line. Farmer works in fluid and quick
movements, slipping down each row as if she's practiced
this dance every afternoon for the last six years.

We separate for lunch. I devour an olive loaf from
Panorama Breads packed with sautéed slabs of fresh
zucchini and wilted lamb quarters, and write a poem
on my laptop under the black locust tree. As I write, a
deer comes within ten feet of my chair; when our eyes
meet, she pauses and then saunters off into the ravine
and across the now dry creek. After lunch, Farmer and I
gather to tackle the irrigation.

Irrigation is the most difficult aspect of our farm work. Farmer bought these heavy metal PVC pipes from another farmer five years ago. Each linkage seems to be missing a latch, sun and heat-worn links never seem to fit right, and the ones that do fit together have no identifying mark—which means that only Farmer can tell which ones work together, and it has taken Baker and I close to three months to situate the links so they don't leak and spray out ten tons of water all at once on one section of the field and drench us in chilly water.

The main water pump, located about 150 feet from our yurt village, supplies the pipes, and can be adjusted for pressure and distance. If we need to water okra in the upper field, we have to open the valve until we hear a deep rumble, which signals the passage of millions of liters of water. If we're watering the eggplants and peppers in the lower field not far from the pump, we open the valve until we hear a slight moan, which might fade into the bustle of birds, wind, and various hopping rodents, only to suddenly become distinct and audible, like the building moan Lily makes when she's spotted a baby bunny.

Instead of a meter or some concrete way of telling how much water gets directed to each field, Baker and I have to feel our way through what too much or too little pressure means. Too little pressure is easy: not much water comes through the network of pipes, and just a trickle survives which won't dampen the desired field. Too much pressure blows the pipe links we just spent an hour trying to assemble and latch, creates indentations in fields, and blows out and drowns transplants before we can drain the pipes and reassemble their connections.

Thankfully, even Farmer has trouble with the irrigation. Since we've all had days when we've cursed the pipes and soaked ourselves to where our underwear would be if we had any, it is natural for one of us to have a fit, get angry and brutally determined to harness the pipes and make them irrigate. So today, as she insists that pipe x meets here with pipe y, and the pressure she sends up to the basil field overwhelms her link, I'm slightly delighted— especially after she gave me a hard time last week when my proposed irrigation network exploded and created a swamp in the okra.

When she smiles her bone-white smile, wrings out her soaked shirt, and laughs about how good the cold water feels against the heat, I am relieved and surprised. Usually an incident with the irrigation makes her mad for hours, and subsequently ruins the afternoon for me as I work alongside her and watch her angrily rip out deeply rooted mallow. For a second I think how happy she looks, and the whole scene in front of me becomes a picture I want to take with me when I retire to the yurt tonight and write. Plum trees all green now, with bold little plum knobs shifting in the slight breeze. Wild lush patches of grass near the permanent sections of irrigation pipe. Dragonflies dart from row to row, their awkward bodies maneuver above the now tall okra stalks. Farmer's joy is so believable and contagious as she seems to mimic the motion of her landscape.

I'm about to say something just to change the strange intimacy I feel toward her, to transition myself out of this moment of connection, when she shakes the excess water out of her hair, looks at me directly, and says:

"So, Baker and I will most likely, hopefully, be in a relationship when this season's ended." She turns away from me and toward the spindly willow trees that line the field's edge. "I don't want..." Farmer stops and looks up into the stark blue sky for words: "I don't want you to feel uncomfortable. I want to do everything I can to make sure you get all you expected out of this apprenticeship."

Lily rushes past us, the fur on her rump supine. Seconds later we hear her bark in the barn, rustle boards, and scratch at something.

"Of course." I say, and smile. "I thought so." I think about what I expected from my time here before I came, which was nothing I could concretely imagine. I just needed a break from working the line every day. To prove to myself that I could love a job that won't wear me down under a knife's edge. I wanted a breakthrough; if not the old me, then another me to emerge.

I can't think what my role is, what she wants from me but to encourage her and tell her it's okay: "I could tell something was going on."

I look up at her expectant face; she's so happy, so

excited.

"I hope things work out between you two," I say, as we turn toward the barn to check on Lily.

July, 2006

Some weekends I stay on the farm and sleep in until the sheets stick uncomfortably to my back, until the stale air compacts and presses against my lungs. I clean up the big mess of dishes and chunks of mud near the door that I've accumulated throughout the week. Sometimes when I water the last few seedlings in the greenhouse, I see Jules cooking in the outdoor kitchen. I read books from my soon to be graduate professors at the local university, write poems, write in my journal, fill the solar shower with water, and clean out the bathtub that when filled with water becomes a deathtrap for lizards. On my day runs in Cold Creek Canyon, green grasses and flowers wither to little blueprints of what they were in the spring. On runs up the hill to the water tower close to the farm, I slip under a barbed wire fence and up a steep gravel road. Cows gather on either side of me, and I test my courage to ignore their steady approaches.

But on these weekends, I mostly think too much. I think about mom's attempt to die, and how I need to live in reference to that event, hold onto all the reasons one might give herself to live. I think about how we each need to sustain, care for our self with the affection a daughter has for her mother, a mother for a daughter.

I think about how if you start to look for reasons to give up, you will find the world stacked against you in a broken washing machine, a week of rain, financial ruin, a friend's death, or a busted tire. I think if you can reverse your thinking, if you can reverse what incidents mean, and make the fact that you are alone, or missed the bus and are now late to work with a cramped foot neutral; if you can do that, and then see reasons to live and hold on in everyday things like tree branches webbed leafless and aligned down a city street, the sun's cast of a clear path for you, steam from street vents making the air tick with the sudden contact of wet heat, then you will be awake to the possibilities. Once you see the possibilities, once you wake up, you will never want to end the self.

I think about Farmer, and how even when it's just us two on the farm she won't leave her motor home; she reads for two days straight. When I see her from afar, she never waves goodbye or says hello, unless I come over to

her and initiate conversation. Even though Farmer and
Baker "most likely will be a couple" when the growing
season ends, Baker still spends every weekend at her
place in the city, and Farmer seems cast adrift in her own
mind the whole time Baker's gone.

I try to leave the farm every other weekend. I drive
into the city and stay with my best friend Janice and her
husband Ricky. They live in an old Victorian in Hayes
Valley, and share the flat with another couple and a
single guy. One room's vacant, so I can crash and not get
in the way too much. On sunny afternoons we picnic on
Baker, Ocean, or Funston Beaches, wade in clear water,
and sleep on blankets near the cliffs. At night, we either
go out dancing at local bars where a friend of a friend
spins record after record, or they watch TV and I walk
the city from Alamo Square to the Mission.

The days preceding my city weekends, I think of all the
possibilities: all the people I might meet in the city; how
each person I encounter might somehow change what I
perceive.

At lunch when I walk back to my yurt, a large mirage

forms between the field's path and the gate to our yurt village, blurs the line between duckweed and seeded amaranth. I long for the ocean's cool-shock and the life smell of seawater, especially as the days get drier, hotter, and routinely crest one hundred degrees.

I've worked it out so that once a month I can afford enough gas to go to the mountains. I pack a cooler with potential sandwich fixings and water, and load my car with a rechargeable lantern and sleeping bag. Just like the weekends that I spend on the farm, most of these traveling weekends contain my thoughts on what I've inherited from my parents, and who I am now and what I want now that the oven's vent rush and tally of orders have left my mind. When I was cooking I didn't have time to stop and think about my next move, except when I decided to leave. Now, what comes next seems so unplanned and unreal: working on the farm and starting grad school in September.

But what comes next becomes me walking up Wawona Falls in Yosemite, snow still clustered at the ridge, hundreds of rainbows forming as the water bangs and

splashes against granite rocks. What comes next becomes
joined bells of blooming Manzanita and my footprints
in evaporating snow. What comes next becomes hours
on the road; my Toyota clicking up once volcanic
mountains; handfuls of walnuts, one hand on the wheel,
as I drive slower than I have ever driven before, try to
look down at shaded streams, meet a squirrel's eye as he
munches on roadside acorns.

I finally reach Lassen, the visitors' center and gift shop
throng with couples and families, and I am alone. I am
only an eye— no feeling of loneliness or isolation left,
but a detachment from need. Or at least that's what I'm
hoping to achieve: "Lose the I," I keep telling myself;
if you could just lose her, you would be okay with the
world set up the way it is, set up with loss and you alone.

I pull into trailhead after trailhead until I find one
empty of cars. A part of me is all fear: something will
attack me, some crazy person or bear, but I'm sick of
feeling fear attached to this female I. I gather my things,
my backpack so full it seems to push me into the ground.
I gather my food inside the car and roll up the windows,

so no bear will eat me when I sleep in the woods. I grip
red pepper spray in my right hand, and go.

I go past the volcanic lake's swap-lilied shore. I cross
tiny wooden bridges and traverse puddles. White star-
like flowers brush my jeans, and I don't feel them. White
pine needles puncture my forearm, but I don't care. I
walk. I go. I climb. Until the sun draws behind the peak.
Until I pass a family. Until the father complains of black
flies, waving his hands frantically in front of his face.
Until I veer off the trail and find a flat patch of ground
that overlooks Lassen Peak. Then I can see the snowcaps
like ruffles on a prom dress glow in the full moon's
light. Then the moon illuminates a valley of lakes and
pines, and a star mimics the moon's light on my right.
Numerous little flies start to nip at my face, tangle into
my hair, bite my sun-ripened farm flesh.

All night I sleep with the bag pulled up to my nose, an
extra shirt over my forehead and eyes, the only exposed
part of me nostrils to take in air — the stupid bugs even
bite my septum. Farmer's idea of sleeping without
anything between you and the stars and moon only

works if there are no bugs around. I curse myself for not bringing a tent, and wake up every time I hear a deer's clomp within ten feet of my sleeping bag. As soon as the sun rises, I get up, pack, and march back to my car.

Virginia, August, 1996

All morning at Monticello's Center for Historic Plants, I fought with the lemongrass, attempted to separate the roots bound like cement to each other and divide the plants into a manageable groups. Jim recently sprayed the greenhouse to kill mites, so I was stuck on transplant duty until the afternoon watering ritual. My nails caked with vermiculite, perlite, Osmocote, and dirt. Every hour I made myself stop transplanting, brought my fingers close to my nose, and inhaled the potting mixture: coco powder and wet moss.

On my break, I smoked a Camel Wide Mouth, and sat on a huge quartz rock. I tried to think of a plot for a story I began last night. This is what I knew about the story: a woman moves to a city, and doesn't realize her neighbors Shelly and Reggie have violent fights, until Shelly ends up in the hospital with a broken arm. My character won't talk to anyone, but she walks the streets, makes up stories of the people she passes. The stories she tells herself about these passers tell us more about her character than anything else. In these stories we realize she is on her way to becoming—now she's only half alive, ticking out her days like a caterpillar in a cocoon.

On these walks, she steals looks at herself in florist or deli windows; her reflection set against delphinium or cases of salami and mortadella. In the early morning she returns to her apartment building and hears thumps coming from Shelly's apartment. She assumes they are having rough sex or foreplay. She makes up a story to rationalize the crash of a plate and the furniture's whine. In the final scene, she stares at herself in a butcher's shop window; in that moment of epiphany she realizes something about herself. I couldn't figure out what she realizes.

From my rock I watched a hilly pasture lined with juniper trees. The hay tips undulated in pre-thunder winds. Dark clouds pregnant with lightening slowly gathered from Charlottesville over the hill. I could spot a mouse tunnel in the red clay, scratch for shelter.

Spring Songs

You sing to the fennel bulb's roots.

All is still in the modulation of notes.

No more silence!

You have mouth.

Small spotted birds speed to the chain fence.

Out from the tree nest.

Out from the feeder filled with flimsy seed husks.

Listen finally to your song.

Let the hemlock shed pollen from budding ends.

Let the rose vines shake petals to the spring wind.

You take them in.

You dig yourself out from day desperation.

Virginia, May, 2004

Was this the beginning?

Jess and I drove down from Charlottesville for the day, past stands of juniper giving way to broad tulip poplars and ash.

What Mom could do to herself scared me. The potential permanence. What she could do and here we were, on Mother's Day, walking down the bright crushed rock roads of Williamsburg. When I was a kid in Maryland, the potential of May made my legs and stomach shake as if filled with fluid about to break, but the daffodils and redbuds close to the old brick buildings here could wilt in a night's frost.

Mom was in rehab for three months; today she was two months in, family day at the center. I still couldn't reconcile what happened and who this woman with the still bruised mouth was in front of me, when for close to twenty-nine years I felt as if I had known her better than I knew myself; I felt I even knew why she got angry when building a chicken coop and her hammer slipped against a nail and ended up bruising her thumb. I seethed with fear of her anger at herself.

We walked the roads too bright in the sunny cool light. This was the second visit Mom was allowed; Dad saw her three weeks ago. Today she was supposed to go through the step that asks for forgiveness from the ones she's hurt. She explained that she was sorry for any pain she had caused us.

We went for brunch at a restaurant crowded with families packed into small booths and waiters carrying crab cake and omelet heavy trays. Women in the other booths wore pink flowery dresses and gel-fancy hair; men wore dark slacks, white button up shirts, and paisley ties. Some tables had bouquets of lilac and baby's breath nestled near the ketchup and Tabasco sauces. We sat in the atrium of the restaurant, and the cool air swirled around my ankles as I ate poached eggs and smoked salmon topped with chives and a hollandaise sauce that needed another squeeze of lemon.

Mom ate clam chowder out of a bread bowl, told us how when her brother Joe died in a car accident during his first year of college she lost all of her faith; she thought God had abandoned her or must not exist. All my life she vacillated between agnosticism and atheism, and now she hinted that she believed in a higher power, that there was a single entity that organized our lives and cared if we got our heads smashed into a windshield, or hammered our own heads with painkillers and vodka. At first I thought this was a script the rehab counselors told her, but as she spoke, still lisping from the seizure's tongue biting and unable to stop staggering her words, I knew it didn't matter, as long as she had a script to explain what she did to herself and that called for a beginning over creamy clam soup.

November, 1968

Mom's brother Joe died on a November night in
Massachusetts, when the first dark weeks crept with cold and
all the leaves were stripped from the trees and an eerie stillness
waited for winter's iron curtain.

This is what I know: it was late, and Joe had fallen asleep on
his dorm bed. His roommate woke him up and asked him to
drive him somewhere. They got in Joe's old Mustang, headed
down a country road. For some reason, Joe didn't stop at a stop
sign, but ran the car straight through the intersection. A car
came from his right and bashed him against the windshield; his
friend got thrown clear through the side. They rushed Joe to the
hospital. Someone called my grandparents, who drove up from
Pennsylvania too late to see him before he died at 3 AM. My
parents were living in Philly at the time and couldn't make it
up to see Joe die.

The friend he was with survived.

This is what I don't know: Why didn't he stop at the stop
sign? Was he drunk, or high, or sleeping off a high, or just tired
from studying? What did he feel or think in those seconds as
the car lights met their fracture on the side of his car? His head

punctured and swaddled in glass; what did he think?

When I think of my mom's most painful loss, I can imagine
how she paused in the utter silence as she returned the dial-up
phone to its receiver in the small apartment she and my dad
had just moved to in Prospect Park. I can imagine her sitting
in the chair in the hall, my dad in the other room studying
his medical books, and the time it takes her to process what
happened enough to get up and speak. I can imagine how
she fought to get through her days at the Vet Hospital; how
every vet from Vietnam with a smashed head and inchoate
eyes reminded her of Joe and how his potential was now held
suspended in the photo of when he and my mom and dad drove
the Blue Ridge Parkway and stopped for burgers near South
River; his smile unbelievably convincing as he landed his arms
around each of my parent's shoulders. I can imagine how
she turned against the belief of possibility inside of her; how
quickly it can be snatched and erased, and how that yearning
to just hug his mass of curly hair and say "Drive carefully"
can haunt a sister who couldn't tell him that because he was six
hours north and eighteen.

Virginia, May, 2004

*On the way back to Charlottesville from Williamsburg, Jess
and I stopped to run on a trail near the York River. No leaves
on the trees, and the earth smelled like decay and soil. After
the density of Californian redwood forests, the deciduous thin
open canopy felt stark and ethereal. Though I'd been back
east for over three months, my childhood landscape was odd
to me, and every skunkweed smell and tulip poplar propeller
triggered a memory from over ten years ago. For the seconds
in between planning my foot fall over ivy tangles and denuded
birch roots, I'd be lost in our childhood fort near the compost
pile that stretched to the quartz-loaded creek; or shooting hoops
alone at the edge of our dead end street, with little tulip poplar
propellers diving down in autumn's dying dance.*

*We did not talk; we ran in complete silence. My script called
for me run into adulthood as the thin tree limbs met above
our heads like unending webs. We ran on single-track trails
that looped and wound down to the York's swampy shores,
hopped over fallen trees, and traversed little creeks that led to
the wide river. Before we got to the shore, as we began to see
the cypress's wide legs swallowed by the river's steady surface,*

a rising and falling insect noise built and built until our ears hurt.

We had to turn back as the rapid clicks got so loud that our eardrums ached and swelled from the pulses.

July, 2006

"You fit into me

Like a hook into an eye

A fish hook

An open eye" Margaret Atwood

A dented trowel. Plastic flat heavy with transplants. Gnats circle my head as I sweat and dig.

Caked and cracked soil: earth an open eye. I'm a fish hook. That's how I fit into the earth. Or is the earth a fish hook, I an open eye?

July, 2006

Food planning. We discuss what we will eat, relish and remember what we just ate. Afternoon breaks, Baker refreshes us with ice cream in the outdoor kitchen: basil ice cream with sun-dried Sungolds; market-traded strawberries from Lodi's Lucero Farms, cooked and swirled in vanilla bean ice cream.

I make pasta, roll out and spread large sheets with my forearms, pass them through the machine for fettuccini, or hand-cut them into thick ribbons for pappardelle. Flour on my shoes. Flour on my workpants. We trade with Ted for cuts of meat he can't sell: goat and lamb shoulder, beef and lamb tongue, odd organ meats that usually sit in the freezer until someone requests them. The last restaurant I worked at, Oliveto, prided itself on using the whole slaughtered animal, and when Baker or Farmer deliver these odd cuts and ask me to cook them, I feel connected and excited to work with something familiar. I know how to build braises from the bottom up: brown shoulder meat, sweat veggies, deglaze with stock and wine, and cook the meat until it's tender.

I can't tell if it is Farmer or Baker's doing, but whereas in the first few months we each went off and did our own thing, now we have family meals. To make me feel included— they don't want me to feel like a third wheel? At least once a week we plan dinners together. Sometimes we plan simple meals like pasta and ice cream, or fried fish and chips. But in late June, with the first flush of tomatoes, the eggplants' bloated bells of flesh, basil leaves tenting out broad, and wild fennel umbrellas turning golden yellow with pollen, we think of a pre-harvest mid-summer eating extravaganza.

We pinch and gather the leafing ends of Egyptian spinach; each tip we place with care into canvas bags. We plan. What's in season here; what can we trade for at market? Baker wants ham; Baker and Farmer want lamb tongue; I want pie and ice cream. What can we use? What's here? I go through lists in my head: what to cook; how to cook it; how to prepare it all in a logical sequence.

Lists of who to invite. Farmer has a following of devoted customers. Harry, a TV producer, comes in his sunhat to the Lake Merritt Market every Saturday and asks what he should buy. Tim and Laurie give Farmer rice and pork sausages from Laurie's Central Valley hometown of Turlock. Each week Farmer smuggles a dozen or so eggs to these, her devotees. These are the people Farmer invites to what the Baker has termed "Christmas in July." I invite my old line-cooking buddy from Oliveto, Ayako, and my friend Betz, who loves to cook and eat. Baker's friend Liz comes in from San Francisco, and Steve and Marj trek over from across the street. A woman who's started a Slow Food chapter, and who raises eggs and olives on a farm a mile away, has also been invited. And of course, Jules should come, if she's not on an archeological dig or staying with her girlfriend in San Francisco. I usually only see Jules just as she's getting up during our coffee breaks, or as she works the bench saw or fixes broken hoes and shovels in exchange for her stay on the farm.

As we cull the Egyptian spinach clean of new growth, I learn that between the invited guests and their friends, we can expect a group of twenty. What to cook? With all these possibilities, what to pick?

According to my calculations, in order for brine to penetrate the meat I need the pork in my hands at least five days prior to roasting. When Farmer brings a huge bone-in ham back from the market frozen, I feel like the brine won't be able to reach the bone in time. I hustle to cook and cool the brine in the outdoor kitchen, and as soon as possible I use my brine injector to infuse the muscle with the sweet and salty aromatic liquid. We have a huge tub, and submerge the ham in the remaining solution and weigh it down with a plate. Four days until roasting.

A few times a day I turn the ham, make sure all flesh gets adequate exposure to the brine. Once a day I take the tub out, feel for any hard still-frozen areas, and inject more brine into the muscles.

The day preceding Christmas, Farmer and I excavate a large hole she dug two years ago for a fish cookout. Apparently, she threw hot coals into the pit, placed a whole fish on a plank, lowered it down into the hole, and covered it in twigs and leaves. Now Farmer insists that the pit needs to be deepened another three feet to stop fire from spreading out of the hole, but I also need the meat to get enough heat to cook at a certain pace. We shovel out dirt, and cross and fix two rebars on either end of the pit. The spitfire at Oliveto had a flame rise in the back of a grill, and the meat would spin close to the heat and away, in a cyclical motion, until it reached temp. I'm skeptical about how our contraption will work, but I hammer the rebars into the sodden earth.

After harvesting Sungolds, eggplant, zucchini, and the first batch of San Marzanos for market the next day, we begin preparations for our party. Last night, I cooked and peeled the lamb tongue and beets; today I make thin slices and layer them on a platter, tangle peppercress against the slices, and drizzle mustard cream in broad swirls. Last night, I slow roasted some Early Girl tomatoes with sea salt and olive oil; today I grill eggplant and zucchini, cool and toss all the vegetables together with fresh basil, Greek oregano, and olive oil. Last night I made a plum mostarda with the plums Farmer preserved last year and some balsamic we traded for at market; today I mix in fresh fennel pollen I've harvested from the corner of Cherry Glen and Pleasants Valley Roads. Today I cut potatoes Farmer picked up at market, lather them in a basil slather, and slow roast them.

But the ham won't cook with the crossed rebars we set up, so I take the bar we skewered through the meat and set it to directly over the pit, hand turn the roast every five to ten minutes to maintain the caramelized crust without too much char. Heat rises from our pit fire, rises from the drying earth as the sun hits past noon; I can see greenness evaporate and give way to summer.

Baker makes her luscious ice cream; as it sets in the freezer, she finishes baking her strawberry upside-down cake. She's very quiet, and her eyes look red and dark beneath, as if she hasn't slept in days. When all three of us work in the fields, I sometimes catch sections of Baker and Farmer's conversations, enough to know that Baker hasn't been sleeping, and she's lucky to get three hours of rest a night.

Farmer spends the hours arranging chairs, setting up water misters in the dining area, chilling beer, and squeezing lemons and grating ginger for her fresh ginger-lemonade. Our guests arrive, but between turning the roast, attending to the grill, cooking, slicing, and plating the food, I don't have time to say more than hello to the group.

When we sit down to eat, I'm reeling and buzzed from preparation and focus; the sudden rush of people leaves me stunned. Lily presses her face to everyone's knee or crotch, intent on convincing each of us to give her some ham. Baker nibbles on her food, talks with Harry and Steve. Farmer sits on the opposite side of the large circle, dangling shreds of meat to call Lily to order.

After dinner, I take my friends on a tour of the place. With pride, I show them the claw foot bathtub I jump in once a day. A lizard lies at the bottom of the clear water, his stiff body awkwardly heavy as I lift him out of the water with a plum branch, throw him over the fence. In the lower field, hot air sits against the tomatoes' fuzzy leaves, fills and expands in the space between rows. We pick a few pints of Black Plum and Green Zebra tomatoes for Betz and Ayako to take home. When the sun sets behind Mount Vaca, I realize my friends will be gone in two hours: I want to go with them.

Back in the outdoor kitchen, Betz and I help Baker plate dessert. Her red shirt wet in pockets from sweat, she looks like she's just recovered from a crying fit and attempts to keep her tears away from display. She gets upset when Betz only takes one plate instead of two to the group, which I can understand when the ice cream pools and soaks the cake.

When Farmer comes into the kitchen, her eyes droop like she's pleading with Baker, but she only says: "Can I do anything?"

Baker looks at her, as if she can't take Farmer's assumption of ignorance, and in a flat, too calm voice says, "No. We're all set."

But we're not—we still have ten plates to prepare and deliver.

Farmer leaves the kitchen; we scoop and lift until Betz comes back and says we're good.

I don't ask Baker anything specific, only "Are you okay?" because I know her agitation has to do with Farmer.

I know whatever goes on between them is not my business, can never become my business. They will sort it out or they won't; regardless, I have to work with both of them until October. Baker's upset, and she's my friend now, so when I see her wipe away her tears, I want to say something. But I don't.

July, 2006

On the way back from market, a highway sign ensnares Farmer; when she arrives at the farm, exhausted from a long selling day, she gets online with her slow dial-up connection. Lily sleeps in a pile of stained t-shirts in the corner. Baker is in San Francisco for the weekend. A quiet mobile home, except for crickets ticking in the ivy that spirals around her gutters. The next day, when we pick huge tomatoes almost splitting from the heat, she reaches under the vines and hands me a neatly folded paper. I unfold her creases; the telltale dirt smudge of Farmer's hand seems to mark the paper before I realize what it says:

2006 Lambtown, USA.

A Celebration of the Lamb Industry in Dixon

Festival & Cook-Off Application and Agreement

She wants us to enter the competition: "Team Tip Top Produce." From what I can tell from the entry form, and from my talk with Farmer, all I need to do is cook lamb — she'll take care of the rest.

I've marinated the Prather Ranch lamb chops in red

wine and olive oil, and spread sliced torpedo onions, thyme, and bay in between each rack. According to Dave, he pastures the sheep out in the grass lands of the Capay Valley, letting the animals get fat on wild grasses and insects. For two days before the festival, each morning and evening I rotate the lamb so the marinade penetrates the meat.

The morning of the cook-off, Farmer loads her truck with a large round grill, a few bags of mesquite charcoal, a bundle of dried plum stems, our vending tent, and our cooler filled with Prather Ranch lamb racks. She's thought of everything: hand towels, worn plastic chairs, lighter fluid, matches, jack cheese and an olive loaf to snack on. Just before we take off, I grab four large bunches of the Persian mint that grows like Samson's hair in front of Farmer's home.

The small town of Dixon lies just twenty minutes west of the farm. Since I can't fit in the front of the truck, I follow in my little Toyota. We barrel down Interstate 80, past verdant orchards' huge tracks and grazing pastures' nibbled grasses. All I can see of Baker: her cowgirl hat; all

I can see of Farmer: her sunhat and her dark arm out the open window to cup clean morning air.

As we enter the fairgrounds, I size up our competition. Eight of the ten contestants have huge BBQ grills, with multiple grilling shelves, rotisseries, and tires that look like they can drive over sand dunes and avalanches. Even their banners flash, bear flaming letters in red and orange with black skewers and cartoon lambs etched to resemble clouds. When we begin to set up, the guy next to us, a candidate for the mayor of Dixon, comes over and tips his baseball cap to the only women in the competition.

For all my years working a grill and cooking roasts, steaks, and sausages, I can't understand why it is considered a macho or manly task to grill meat; I take pride in the fact that I can marinate, grill, lift heavy grates, and stand the flaming charcoal just as well, if not better, than any man.

Farmer, Baker, and I unload the pickup truck. Farmer has a particular idea of how to set up our station, and rather than get in her way, Baker and I go to the bathroom and look for coffee. Ranchers who've brought their best sheep in for show have already set up temporary stalls, and the fairgrounds smell of hay and dung mixed with the aroma of frying funnel cakes and cotton candy. Lone workers sweep the pavement near each food booth; their brooms usher hay tips, popsicles sticks, and candy wrappers into dustbins.

"Lamb Taco," "Deep Fried Snickers," and "Red Hots" in black ink on cardboard or trumpeted on shiny signs, draw me into the festive spirit, and I can't wait until lunch so I can figure out what a lamb taco is. I haven't been to a festival since I left the east coast; now I'm transported into a dreamy state by food memories of funnel cake and sausage with peppers and onions, served from large vending trucks at the church bazaars I used to haunt with my cousin on Pennsylvanian summer nights.

When we arrive back at our tent, Farmer has dialed our station in, and every detail except the arrangement of cutting boards and salt and pepper shakers has been attended to. The circular grill sits out in the makeshift alley between tents, close to the mayoral candidate's monstrous BBQ machine. She's even set the charcoal and plum twigs so we just have to drop a match down and flames will rise.

For the next hour, I make salsa verde to spoon over the lamb once it is grilled. I mince shallots and place them in a small ceramic container with market-sourced red wine vinegar and a hefty pinch of sea salt. For the next phase of salsa production, I take the just-harvested Persian mint, slice it into thin ribbons, turn the ribbons 45 degrees to my left, and slice them into tiny squares. As soon as I finish cutting each batch, I submerge the sliced mint in herbaceous and buttery extra-virgin olive oil we procured from market. To this olive infusion I add another hefty pinch of sea salt, a few turns of fresh cracked pepper, and a tablespoon of chopped capers. I let each of these sauces develop for another two hours, pull the racks out of the marinade, light the grill, and wait until right before judging to cook the chops.

Baker has invited her friend Liz to meet us at the festival; they walk around sampling wares. Farmer concentrates on the unnecessary organizing of our station, and reads her history book on the Middle East under our tent's shade. I wander the festival lanes, get a free toothbrush, check out my weight, wait in line for a free foot massage, watch sheep shearing contests, and eat a lamb taco. The lamb taco isn't a taco at all, but canned salsa, sour cream, orange cheese, ground browned lamb, and Cool Ranch Doritos crunched and served in their bag. I feel a little heartburn make itself into my esophagus after eating the lamb taco, but I'm so hungry I get another bag o' crunch. I wonder what this would taste like with regular Doritos and some black beans. I wonder what this would taste like sprinkled on iceberg lettuce, or what would happen if I took out the ground lamb, and added thin grilled lamb loin, topped with this confetti of dairy, tomato, and onion.

After what seems like a long wait in which we could have hunted, slaughtered, butchered, and roasted a whole lamb, we get the word that we have a half hour before we present our dish. I brush the racks with olive oil, season them with salt and pepper, and place them on the grill. Each turn yields a caramelized crust; each time I touch the meat it gets firmer and firmer, until it feels like the flesh between my thumb and index finger when I gently bring them together. I take the brick-red browned racks off the heat, and let them rest as the grilled lamb smell billows into my nose. I mix the shallot-vinegar with the mint infusion, wait another four minutes, and cut each rack into big chops, while Farmer arranges the numerous chops on a platter, spoons unctuous mint salsa verde over each meat morsel, and tops the platter with a few pinches of sea salt. We're so hungry, as soon as we send the platter off to the judges, Farmer and I sit down to eat a rack each.

When Farmer and I get back to the farm, I jump out of my car, unlock the gate, remove the chain, and pull open the wide chain link doors. She speeds in with her truck, kicks up dust into the cricket-loud air as I pop back to my car and drive in. Baker has headed into San Francisco with Liz for the weekend, so Farmer and I unpack the truck dirty with the remnants of our grilling. Charcoal residue collects in the ridges of her truck's bed, coats the grill cast on its side and our white vending tent, and makes our tongs and knives dirtied with bits of lamb crust and hardened juice look like the tools of a coal miner.

We're silent the whole time we unload and pass objects to one another as in an assembly line. We're too tired to put everything away properly, so we stack the tent and the grill just under the roof of the onion drying shed. When we're finished, I'm about to head back to my yurt to write and lie down on the futon, but Farmer says: "Hey, Cheffy—"

She reaches into her jean pocket, unfolds an envelope with the five hundred dollars of Lambfest prize money and hands it to me. I thank her, and she pauses to look at the edge of the drying shed, its planks sticking out like they will fall off at any minute.

"I got Harold and Maude from Netflix and was going to watch it...do you want to watch it with me?" Her blue eyes still flash through her tiredness, through her charcoal and sun-worn skin; the contrast makes her look like an awkward girl not sure how to ask another kid to play with her.

I pick up our plaque announcing our first place finish in

the cook-off, and follow her into her mobile home. She's makes popcorn, and loads the DVD into her machine smudged with soil. I lie on the couch shrouded in a white bed sheet, and immediately Lily jumps up and wedges her warm little body and fast heartbeat under my knees. My big toe rises and falls with her breathing. Farmer sits in the chair draped with a pink floral sheet. She stacks her legs under her body at first, as if pressing her knees into the chair and her torso before extending them and slouching toward the wood floor.

Maude commits suicide at the end of the movie by taking a bottle of sleeping pills on her eightieth birthday. She is not sad or upset. Maude decided: "Eighty seems like a good number." Harold is livid, rushes Maude to the hospital, screams at her to stay awake.

"I love you Maude," Harold says to Maude in the hospital bed.

"That's wonderful Harold. Go out and love some more." Then Maude smiles, her lips push against the wrinkles on her face before they relax in death.

This end always makes me cry; it made me cry the first

time I saw the movie with my high school friends Katie
and Jazz, and when I saw it stoned out of my gourd after
smoking a hit through a six-foot bong. But I'm never sure
whom I am crying for: Harold or Maude.

When I look over I see Farmer crying too. Through
the flash of her eyes reflecting the screen, I can see she's
caught in the same thought cycle as I am. For a second,
I step out of my crying and know we're both thinking of
our mothers, not Harold or Maude.

GABRIELLE MYERS

Virginia, July, 1995

Manicured golf lawn. Little ponds swelled with thunderstorm water. Crabgrass-split parking lot asphalt. Bacon cheeseburgers at the Club's café: old men and young men and green golf pants and yellow polo shirts and grass-worn clubs.

Mom convinced me to putt some rounds with her at the public golf course. We were less than four suburban blocks from the townhouse Dad and her moved to the year before from Maryland. I lived closer to downtown and UVA with my college friend, Shimiah, in an apartment we rented at $650 for the whole summer. Because of my sparse attendance during my first year of college, I only finished four out of six classes. My parents refused to help pay for any more school. I took two classes at UVA's summer school to make up my credits. No more fucking around. No more trips to New Orleans or Kentucky or Boston during the school week.

I didn't like golf and how elite it seemed, but my mom always loved to get out on the green for the afternoon with her friends and colleagues.

I hated most of my life now, except reading, writing, smoking cigarettes, and smoking weed until I coughed for five minutes

128

and then reached the still stare state where I could sit and look at a wall and feel elation in my heart's fluttering beat.

Working as a waitress at Aunt Sarah's Pancake House was okay because of the free staff lunches which we could order off the menu: pancakes, scrambled eggs, Virginia ham, grilled cheese, club sandwich, or French fries. It was okay working there until the weekend manager's boyfriend trapped me in a "I'm gonna' get you dance" in the narrow soda fountain and ice tea machine section; after which Amy, my trainer, told me that every woman working in the restaurant had to deal with Larry's flirtations, and the best that I could do was ignore him, since he was harmless when it came down to it.

I actually was getting into the hang of the job, which consisted of taking orders, filling drinks like coffee and soda, making salads, and taking scheduled breaks to smoke and drink coffee with Amy, until a woman with a roving left-eye and pooled sweat from the humid one-hundred degree day sat in my section and ordered ice tea. When I asked her if she wanted anything else, she said she was just fine with the tea, but maybe she'd look at the menu. I went to other tables and ran to get plates of club sandwiches and trays filled with coffee and soda, and when I checked on her seven minutes later she said I had forgotten about her; I was rude, and she was sick of waiting for me. She put $1.55 down in change for the tea and walked out.

I began to hate my job that night as I got off work and drove the mile back to the apartment. I smoked a cigarette and took a sip from my one-hitter. All the neon chain restaurants blurred into the little neon blue, red, and silver sketch of Aunt Sarah and her broom.

Later that week I began to hate the way that humidity created a thin bubble and weight over my thick curly hair—how it hung onto my high thoughts and made them feel heavy and loaded to the grey carpet in our apartment. I hated the way I felt: a worn out balloon, wrinkled and sunk and ugly at nineteen. I was on my third antidepressant and it wasn't working. I started having panic attacks after the second week of starting Wellbutrin; I was scared to leave the apartment and called in sick to my job at Aunt Sarah's two nights in a row.

I don't know how she did it, but Mom convinced me to putt some rounds with her. She told me to stand with my knees bent, how to hold my arms packed with energy as I swung back the putter, how to swing with the same sense of follow through *that you try with a baseball bat. The humidity rested around our ears and made the shots of other golfers crack and dissipate so quickly we couldn't tell who had swung the ball heading for tulip poplars or wooden ducks. I keep missing the hole, and after ten minutes I got frustrated, lost interest in the game, and sat at a table in the cafe looking at a menu of burgers and sandwiches.*

I don't know what happened next—what we said or talked about. I only remember we were in her Ford Explorer, high above the pavement splitting crabgrass. Mom was driving. The soundtrack to Grease played the "We go together like shebang whingdeedigdedong" song, and Mom said: "Why does everyone have to be so fucking sad all the time?"

I wasn't sure I had heard her right, said "What?" I looked at her and then down at a coffee cup rolling around on the floor.

Her large brown eyes left the road and met mine and I knew she'd been holding something down: "You and your dad and your sister, everyone is so sad and depressed all the time. Why does everyone have to be so fucking sad all the time?"

Her voice like an Iraqi woman whose son was blown up in a bomb two years ago. Her voice like my religion teacher's from

*high school, asking a bunch of sixteen year-olds why Kitty
Genovese's neighbors didn't respond to her shouts.*

  *I imagined John Travolta and Olivia Newton swinging
each other among ankle-high blue jeans and knee-low skirts,
and their smiles: their teeth white and eyes sincere. I tried
to imagine my dad and sister and even my mom being that
convinced in their happiness, or in their relationship with
another person. I tried to imagine them jumping on hot rods
and smiling too long. I couldn't fit them into the smile; and
this thought felt familiar, like it was a line from a poem or story
I had read but couldn't remember apart from my thoughts.*

  *I don't remember what I said to her. Maybe: "I don't
know," and looked out the window at the tame and deforested
suburban hills as we drove back to their townhouse. But here's
what I thought and will never forget: how I feel can become
how someone else feels.*

July, 2006

Farmer and I eat. Today, with Baker at the Berkeley Market, we decide to go into Vacaville for lunch. Farmer wants a hamburger. She's decided to quit smoking her rolled cigarettes, and has started taking a drug she ordered online that's suppose to curb her need for nicotine, but apparently it fuels her hunger instead. I want grilled ham and cheese, made with processed American cheese that runs out of the crisped bread, warm and delicate. After we finish our after harvest duties of sweeping the packing barn and putting away any unused boxes, we hop into her truck. I push crumpled and fanned seed catalogs over with my left foot so I can place both feet on the floor, and gather white plant tags strewn over my seat and place them in the dashboard's depression.

Farmer drives fast past the bee boxes, ancient fig trees, plum orchards, and empty fields that line Bucktown Road. The turn onto Vacaville Way always seems awkward to me—the fields and rural hum of tractors and birds suddenly give way to new grandiose suburban houses, and before we know it, we are surrounded by shopping plazas, gas stations, and low office buildings. Farmer needs to stop off at the local hardware store, so we pull into a small parking lot empty in the weekday afternoon heat. She jumps from the truck and saunters into the store. I stay in the truck, read through her warped Terrain Seed Catalog, watch a mirage rise from the blacktop and make the seeded grasses at the edge of pavement look like they're melting into the air.

The Corner Diner is literally shaped into the corner of Mason and Merchant Streets in historic downtown Vacaville: where two streets meet, the white stucco forms dramatic edged walls. Inside the joint, the dining counter models itself after the exterior's corner, like a half triangle, the counter faces the kitchen window. I think I've been in the Bay Area dining scene too long, because my first thought as we walk in is a complete fantasy of buying the place and turning it into a 'campy' retro diner featuring locally produced foods. The senior daytime lunch crowd eyes us in our dirt-stained and torn farm apparel before the waitress takes us to a booth overlooking Mason Street.

The menu has little graphics of purple ice cream sundaes, yellow and black French fries, and compressed hamburgers arranged in between the menu options. The waitress takes our order, brings our drinks, and we sit across from each other, both at a loss of what to say, but beyond the point of paying too much attention to our silence. I want to ask about Jules, because I haven't seen her around much, and when I do see her she's sipping cans of Bud and smoking. Last time I saw her and Farmer in the outdoor kitchen I was in the greenhouse, finishing up watering the okra that's now in the fields. I saw their movements through the shade cloth's opening. Farmer lowered her brows, said something to Jules, waved her hand, and walked off toward the barn. Jules just looked down at the gravel beginning to bake in the afternoon heat.

"I haven't seen Jules around—what's she been up to?" I blurt out as Farmer and I make eye contact for the third time in silence.

She looks down at the white table, runs her right

hand toward her napkin and silverware, and begins to speak like she's practiced these sentences in her head. She doesn't look up at me until she's finished: "I'm thinking of asking her to leave the farm. Her drinking has gotten outta' control, and she's not finished building the composting structure like we agreed—it's been over a year. And there are other projects she's left undone."

Farmer picks up the butter knife and runs her thumb across the small serrations; her thumb turns red from the pressure: "It's just hard. We go way back. We've been friends for fifteen years, and I've seen her not act this way. I keep thinking she'll stop, but after the last year I think I'm just making it too easy for her to keep drinking."

After my year of Al-Alnon and AA meetings, a part of me feels like I can support Farmer's decision, but another part of me thinks back to right before Mom took her handful of pills, when she drank as if the vodka held an essential piece of herself she tried to get back. Her rages and drinking escalated until Dad had to force her out of the family business, because she refused to admit she drank too much, refused help. While I'm not convinced making Jules move will lead to anything, I don't see her staying on the farm as a good situation for her or for Farmer.

"It might be best for her, in the long run. Maybe it will act like a wake up call," I say, and look directly at Farmer. The blood vessels in her eyes have begun to redden, become more pronounced.

"Yeah. I just don't know what else to do. We can't continue like this any longer. The thing is, when our friend Chris died, all we had was each other. I just feel like I'm abandoning Jules, and…" Farmer turns her head to the window, and I turn as well, watch as a retired couple makes their way toward the dining entrance. The tall lean old man's back has the bend of age, and his wife, who's stout and hefty, seems to hold him up as they mount the sidewalk. "It's just that Chris was really important to the both of us, and her death was hard."

I try to look in Farmer's eyes, but they must be tearing up, because she turns her head completely to the window: "The five year anniversary of her death is in

September."

I don't know what to say, but know I have to say something to make Farmer feel better: "Maybe you will be doing Jules a favor. Maybe she won't get better until she hits rock bottom. Maybe you have to let her."

Before Farmer can respond our food arrives. The waitress can barely hold the heavy load of sandwiches, fries, and coleslaw, and as she delivers my plate a stray fry lands on the table and slides toward the window. We're both so hungry we immediately pick up our sandwiches and begin chewing. I feel the warm butter and cheese oil slip down my chin and pause to bring the napkin to my mouth. Hamburger juice and grease runs at a steady trickle down Farmer's chin as she devours her burger, pauses only to sip her soda or chomp a fry. Our conversation fades as we both concentrate on our food, glance out at the early afternoon traffic, and think.

I think about Chris: from what the Farmer has said today and during our planting-weeding-harvest talks, I wish I had known her. Farmer's devoted to her memory, and anyone who's had a big influence on Farmer must

be brilliant and speak beyond her own life and situation.
Farmer is smart and doesn't take bullshit from people—
even if it's well intended bullshit.

Chris was a photographer; she worked in the industry
before people realized how dangerous the chemicals
were. Apparently they didn't use gloves, just dipped
their hands into the solutions to grab their photos.
She died slow and painful, everyone hoping the next
treatment would work—and it did for a while, until the
cancer spread like a fungus under the surface of her skin,
bloomed beyond each membrane and into her bones.

I guess Farmer thinks about Chris and loss and Jules
and how time rushes you forward like waves push
spilled oil, disconnected buoys, and shattered beer bottles
on shore.

But I'm probably wrong. She wipes the burger juice
from the plate with her last French fry. "We need to
hurry up now. When we get back I'm putting you on
tying the Christmas limas to the next level and harvesting
the black-eyed peas—I need to do some tractor work,"
she says, but not before she lets out a guttural burp and

gulps her soda.

Okra

In the early dew her pants soak,
thighs itch from fine leaf hairs.
Her latexed hands hold and twist the hard ridges,
pull them from their bond with the stalk.
Too many turn wooden,
she can't pick the long seeded fruits quickly enough.

Fragile shell-sides bruise,
each one in its lined box,
torn stems arranged in rows, carried
like children to the packing shed.

Tonight she fries and eats
golden disk by disk,
until oil and seeds bubble in the back of her throat
—burn pop swallow burn swallow water water.

Four of the twelve farm rows planted.
Red Burgundy. Cajun Delight. Cow Horn. Alabama Red.
Tall green and red spires spear the valley air.

Foodies refuse to pay more than two-fifty a pint
for slimy gumbo sliding down.

All night she hears their pods snap beneath her boots.

July, 2006

Maybe because she's so inaccessible, Farmer has already taken on a fictitious role in my mind. We get to know each other, and then she does something to confound that knowing; always she edges away, to where she's unreachable. I must make her up.

I want to shout over the bending and twisting vines: "We never lose our inaccessible parts, do we?" But of course, I don't say anything; I just continue to pull and pluck tomatoes, some of which burst through their thin skins, sting my cracked fingers with their juice.

Pennsylvania, 1984

Branches fat with fruit hung toward the clipped lawn. Bees swarmed around us, took golden dust onto their legs. Grandpa bounced by on the sit-down lawn mower he just bought. Grandma, Jessie, and I picked blueberries at the bottom of the hill. The summer before we lost to the deer, but this summer we picked early, nabbed the premature berries before the bucks got their teeth over our spiny branches.

Since seven in the morning Grandpa was busy: clipping the grape and raspberry vines, spraying the peaches, fertilizing the perennial flowerbed, and mowing the acre and a half of lawn. The lawn sloped to the valley, and I loved running down the hill to the blueberries, even if I only saw the naked nubs of the blueberry branches.

Years later, when Grandpa was catatonic in the Heritage House nursing home, Grandma pointed to this day as the start of Grandpa's decline. Though his colleagues claimed he had had an allergic reaction to a bee bite, Grandma was convinced that he experienced his first stroke that day.

We rushed to the hospital from their hilltop, Grandpa barely conscious in the passenger's seat, Jess and I stuck to the black

*vinyl in the back. The birches that always look like skeletons
in winter were flush with the razor tips of numerous leaves.
Now, I imagine the leaves cut the humid air, pulled the pollen
into their green claws, divided and silenced the crickets that hid
under rocks.*

July, 2006

This happens next: Gina Smith. This happens next:
I wake up to a warm summer morning; the dew
evaporates a little slower now, and carries potential with
it up the first set of tomato leaves, through each level
of green, and out the ends of all the fruits that ripen
simultaneously to my right and left. I walk to the outdoor
kitchen's dinning table, and see Gina. As soon as I talk
with her and hear her voice, something turns inside me—
something turns out.

One of Baker's best friends from Boston, Gina arrived
last night from Atlanta, where she grew up and where
she was living with her folks for a few months. For a
few days, she's staying in the old camper between our
two yurts. For the past week, Baker's told us stories of
the funny things Gina would do as they rolled dough
or sprinkled cinnamon on crispy pastries. Today we're
taking Gina to the Yuba.

The next few days blur, because I'm astounded by the
fact of Gina. I'm in shock, and each step I take along the
Yuba's pine-soft trail becomes measured, defined, and

of unbelievable importance. I walk with Gina and Baker
as Farmer and Lily lead us to our swimming beach and
the broad granite slabs that act as our sun-chairs. I don't
know what I'm saying in response to her statements, or
even what Baker says.

Gina asks about the twisted reddish-barked bush, "The
one with the elongated coin-shaped leaves."

Baker or I answer "manzanita," and Gina repeats the
word "manzanita" twice in her sweet Georgian accent,
like an incantation.

Gina says the Sierras give you a different feeling
than the Appalachians. The Sierras have openness,
expansiveness that makes you feel small, while the
Appalachians crowd you tight in folding ravines and leaf
cluttered trails. I agree, but I can't tell if I've only thought
and not said how the smallness makes you untethered
and inconceivable—for moments you can forget all the
limits your mind erects, and be in a pine standing erect
to the blue sky. For a moment I miss the leaf rush and
density of the Appalachians—how walking under tulip
poplar canopies we are confronted with life and death at

the same time.

When we get to the river the turquoise water isn't as high as it was when we made our last trip; the water seems thicker, suppler as it wraps itself around glittering boulders, lingers for a moment before rubbing a small beach and feeding aspen roots that jut on the shore's edge. We unload our bags and take off our tops, use our shorts as swim trunks. According to Farmer, parts of the South Yuba are considered nude friendly, so we don't give two thoughts to our half nudity.

I'm the first in the water; I let my body suspend in the river's forward motion as I anchor to a jagged rock with my right hand. Gina lowers herself into the still chilly water between two boulders, and then submerges herself in a deep pool. When she surfaces, she clears the water from her eyes, and shakes her long hair like a dragonfly shimmying her wings so she can maneuver over a still lake. She swims in another pool calm from two boulders heading off the river's rush, and I'm compelled to swim in the pool with her. Her straight brown hair curls around her thin muscular shoulders, and I don't know what I'm saying or asking, just establishing contact with her seems like my task. My major task for the whole summer. If I can speak with Gina, then I will have accomplished something from my lonely meanderings in Lassen and Yosemite.

Gina tells me about the school she will attend in Seattle, the new life she's excited to begin. She worked for landscaping companies in Boston and in Atlanta, and now she's on her way to graduate school in landscape architecture. She likes street art too, and we talk about the sculptures we remember from various cities, how each sculpture draws people to marvel at its detail, oddness, or immensity—but we never have the cities in common, so we're not clear on the physicality of the other's sculptures.

The rest of the day we lounge by the river. Farmer and Baker sit close on a rise of boulders, while Gina wanders down the river's edge to take pictures. I'm rereading *Ariel* by Plath. I sit on the edge of a boulder, and every so often I dip in the river to sting myself awake.

I try to write a poem mimicking Plath's detailed

precision and off-the-hook use of figurative language, but the poem only resembles Plath in its fascination with death. I'm writing about my grandmother's funeral. My mom's mom died of heart trouble, and in her last days, she was in a nursing home not far from the mountain lake we use to play in when we visited Pennsylvania during the summer. In the nursing home, she looked thin, like a victim of famine; her lips blue from lack of oxygen.

Grannie's death was my first death, besides our family dog, King, who died when I was in ninth grade. When I saw Grannie in the funeral home, covered in makeup, and adorned with all the jewelry she wore when she was alive, it didn't freak me out so much as etch itself into the imagery of my brain. Grannie didn't feel dead to me—not until Uncle John couldn't get Grannie's ring off before they loaded her casket on the hearse for the cemetery trip. He pulled and struggled with the huge rock and thick glittery band; his face turned red through dried tears.

Why was it stuck like that? As if to remind them that

she would take something physical and material with her when she left? Something about that action's effort made Grannie's death real. The ring left an indentation around her finger; a tract of red skin led up to her nail.

Just before I finish the last line of my poem, Lily comes up to give me a big kiss on the knee; she wags her tail as if she's about to take flight toward Burger King. I hear a laugh, and look over to see Gina's smile and river-wet body. From my boulder, I can see she's sketched a detailed picture in thin blue ink: Lily perched on a rock and the sinuous river trailing behind each boulder.

July, 2006

What happens next: I become a fool who idealizes and adores every word or look Gina produces from her passenger's side car seat. On our way back from the Yuba, we stop at a gas station; I watch how she walks casually to the bathroom, and energetically pays for her snack, gracious to the guy working the counter. When she offers me roasted sunflower seeds, I take a big handful, even though I'm not hungry. When she asks questions about eucalyptus and valley oaks, I answer her in as much detail as I can, hoping to sound knowledgeable about the landscape, hoping that she'll see my ability to name buckthorn as a sign that we'd make a great couple.

The following day, all four of us harvest Sungolds, Purple Plums, Green Zebras, San Marzanos, and Black Cherokees. In the heat, I'm quiet and dazed listening to Gina and Baker. Every once in a while Farmer pitches in to keep the conversations flowing. Farmer seems actively interested in Gina, and in moments like these I can see how much Farmer cares for Baker: she's willing to step outside of herself to befriend Gina, because Gina is Baker's close friend.

I only speak to ask Gina questions, not sure how to establish a connection with her. I ask about the landscaper she worked for in Atlanta, what kind of photographs she takes, why she chose Seattle. The only other time I speak for the whole afternoon is when Gina directly asks me questions, usually in response to the question I just ask her, or in reference to a question Baker or Farmer asks. A part of me wants to believe she's interested in me, that's why she's asking me questions; when I try to pin our conversation down I see nothing that points to her overwhelming passion for me—just friendly response and conversation.

Twice during the afternoon, Lily has heard a bunny or mouse in the brush that edges our tomato field, and a subsequent loud screech interrupts our human banter. In the silence between our words the crickets, slower and more lethargic as the dry season extends into each grass tip, sound their calls irregular and weak. At five, we break to relax before we all meet back at the communal kitchen.

During our break I clean up as best as I can: I wash my face with the cold tap water in my yurt and brush my teeth, pick out my toughest looking tank top to show my biceps and strong forearms. I stride through the field, try to look sure and confident as I pass onion spears and stop at okra standing like spires in the dense early evening heat. I snap a few pods of young and tender Burgundy Delight and Cow Horn, and continue my definite walk to the communal kitchen.

When I get to the kitchen, the sun's started to angle itself at Mount Vaca. The golden light casts a reddish filter on my knife work as I thinly slice the halibut fillet, fish so fresh the white flesh looks slightly blue and feels sturdy under my knife. After I cut the halibut into tiny cubes, I place it in a stainless steel bowl on top of an ice bag, grate a pinch of lemon zest, sprinkle sea salt, and mix in a good amount of olive oil. All the time I maneuver around the kitchen's gravel floor and awkward cutting boards that jut over the table at weird angles, I think of Gina and how she is here, on this farm.

And I'm here too.

That simple fact rolls over in my mind, and the combination of us both inhabiting the same space seems like an unreal gift. I wait to slice the paper-thin disks from the okra I gathered. I sit at the table and read last month's edition of the *Vacaville Times* warped and bent from the sun until it looks like the gravel my feet press into.

Farmer arrives with a large tray filled with ginger, lemon juice, vodka, and a few glasses sweating with ice. She's showered and put on her white tweed pants and a fresh t-shirt. Her teeth look starched and bleached paired with her clean pants. She walks into the kitchen and looks down at my tartare.

"Oh, Cheffy, that looks good! Can I do anything?" Farmer begins to mix ginger and fresh lemon juice with vodka. Her tan hands work quickly to set each glass around the table, and she hands me a glass dripping from condensation. I accept the drink, but at first I hesitate, a little scared.

Last year, I stopped drinking for nine months. Since

staying on the farm, I've had a total of five drinks, generally beer consumed when I'm in town visiting Janice and Ricky. I seem to be okay—I'll have a beer and not really think about having another one for several weeks. I'm beginning to see that my mom's alcoholism is not mine. But I'm still fearful of what I might become and this haunts me through every sip.

Baker walks across the herb circle to the kitchen; her leg brushes a tarragon plant the size of a small citrus tree.

We each do our bit of tidying, and set the table. Gina arrives smiling, flush and tan from her day in our fields. I begin to disk the okra with my sharpest knife. I gently mix the tartare and arrange a thin circular layer on each plate. I distribute five disks of okra on each circle, drizzle extra virgin olive oil over the whole plate, and sprinkle wild fennel pollen that I harvested near Lake Berryessa last weekend over the tartare.

Tartare: beef, lamb, tuna, halibut; all I have to do is cut, season, pair it with a good olive oil and garnish. The tender, fragile quality of the meat or fish plays against the texture present in each bite. Tartare was my favorite dish to serve at Oliveto. We'd fry capers until they were stiff star-like flowers, or take nasturtium petals and dot them over eye of round, ground and moist with oil so the dish looked like a Monet painting.

We eat and I'm nervous that Gina won't like raw fish, but she does, and everyone seems happy, so I'm happy. The crickets have begun to pick up as the sun turns down below Mount Vaca; they seem to work themselves into frenzy as night begins this time of year, only to mellow out as the dark hours progress.

Baker has made delicate basil ice cream studded with sun-dried Sungolds. The dried morsels have the chewy texture of raisins, but retain the acidic leap of Sungolds and work to balance the cream's richness. The basil pairs well with the halibut's sublime flavor, and my taste buds swim with the combination.

Gina asks us questions about what we've made, and she seems genuinely interested in our processes. She and Baker discuss their trip to the city tomorrow, and we each mention places in San Francisco Gina should see before she heads up to Seattle. I plan to arrive in the city the following day, when Gina and Baker will be on their way back to the farm. Last week, I made plans with Janice and Ricky to catch a ride to Tahoe for a concert by Ricky's band. But now I wish I had an excuse to see Gina again.

We finish our drinks, sip until the ice melts and mixes with the alcohol. Baker, Gina, and I walk down to the yurt village, and Farmer and Lily head to sleep. As we're walking, I don't say anything, just smile and nod when it seems appropriate. I'm thinking about how odd life is; how you can be alone for most of your life, and then suddenly meet someone and all that past seems like someone else's past, and your former self becomes a character you view from afar. In the back of my mind, I hope that Gina is the person to make my past self strange to me, but when we get to our yurts I know there's no time. I hug her. She hugs me back. I tell her it was great to meet her. I hope she has an awesome time in Seattle.

Gina says: "It was great to meet you Cheffy! Come visit me in Seattle sometime!"

I'm too stunned to reply with more than a big smile and

an "I will."

Gina and Baker head to Gina's camper van, our fancy guest quarters. The crickets have calmed down, and the hum of Gina's voice fills the space in between cricket calls. Her smile cements itself into my mind as I drift to sleep.

Maryland, 1993

Eighteen and I'm drunk on shot-gunned Meister Brau and

Mad Dog 20/20: Kiwi-Strawberry. My parents left me alone

for the weekend when they flew up to Boston for a conference.

Blankets and friends in the backyard, near the creek. When

the Metallica or Black Sabbath or Guns and Roses' song ends, I

can hear crickets bleat from the edge of the creek. I just broke up

with Phil, and to make him jealous I begin to hit on my friend

Mike's younger brother. He's only sixteen, but I slip my hands

beneath his shorts and through his boxers. Suddenly, there's

just his hardness and my mouth. When I look up, my friends

are gone, but the cricket chorus ascends like the finale to Tosca.

August, 2006

The next day Farmer and I work the tomatoes again, for the third time this week. Monotony has begun to set in, but I hold off fantasizing about Gina until I pluck the thousandth tomato from the vine and pack my sixtieth pint into the fifth flat. Farmer's got her iPod attached to her belt and white earphones on her head, so I'm free to create scenario after scenario of my next meeting with Gina. Maybe this winter she'll come visit Baker in the city, and we'll go to the SFMOMA and look at a photography exhibit together. I'll say something casual and offhand about a photo, and she'll look at me and fall in love. Or she'll visit around Thanksgiving, and I'll roast the turkey so perfectly that the juiciness and crisp skin will cause her to raise a wine glass to toast the meal—we'll make eye contact, and the vibrations will slowly start to overwhelm her heart.

The truth is I've watched too many soap operas. For huge chunks of my childhood I was deeply concerned about whether Robert and Anna could save their marriage. Did Luke really love Laura enough to stop his dangerous dealings? My grannie welcomed me to the imaginary world of drama when I was still a young girl. She came down from Pennsylvania to take care of us while my folks were on vacation for two weeks. I clearly remember coming home from third grade, exhausted from trying to fit in with the popular group and lose my tomboyish twitches of behavior. Grannie had moved our big twenty-inch TV into the dining room. Stacks of silverware and plates lined the dining room table, evidence of Grannie's rearranging and her subtle frustration with my mom's career-minded housekeeping.

A large bowl of Fritos nestled close to Grannie's right hand, and she invited me to sit with her and watch her show. I was only allowed to watch TV on the weekends, so Grannie's offer seemed like a bag of mint chocolates I would be stupid to refuse. The next hour signified my entry into a world of explosive cars, illegitimate children, and twisted love affairs so exciting and passionate that for the next twenty years the reality of actual love would seem mundane, and slightly disappointing.

At thirty, I'm still not out from under the grip of

melodrama, and all my actual sexual affairs have paled in comparison to my imaginative forays. Never have the sex and romance worked out in any satisfying way—at least not yet. When I was a stoner and a drinker, I was the queen of unspoken crushes, but the sex part seemed easy enough. There were always guys who wanted to get laid, even if it might take twice around before I realized that was all they really wanted. I had fallen in deep unrequited love with another friend, but I never worked up the courage to kiss that friend or confess my love until she'd found a serious girlfriend. Too late, I told myself, I might as well stick to sex and forget the whole love thing.

But since I've been sober, the sex I've had has felt strangely intense for the women or men I end up sleeping with: the who or why of sex has slowly started to matter again, like it did when I was sixteen and a virgin. The scene where violins play, where the frosted lens makes reality seem like we're in a dream, only we're in a field and the sun's set, and stars have come out as if brought down to signal our coupling: there's a part of me that still expects this to happen.

August, 2006

The truth is, no matter who you are, someone can fall in love with you. That is reality. Even Eichmann was loved by someone.

Possibility pulls itself down to swim through every vein of a plum leaf when I imagine Gina's sketch of the river, how she took care to shade in the dark belly of each rock. Now all the sex and crushes that dot my past momentarily become swept up in Gina's glance and pen-stroke.

August, 2006

My day off. I sleep until I hear a fly trapped and hitting the yurt's canvas in a perpetual cycle that's lasted at least ten minutes. It's so hot that I'm naked and still sweating where my body touches the bedding. My cell phone says ten-thirty, and I need to be in SF by twelve-thirty to meet up with Janice and Ricky for our Tahoe trip. I stuff clean city clothes in my backpack, make coffee, and double-check to be sure all the propane for the stove is turned off. I speed walk through the field that last night rang with a thousand crickets and Gina's voice; now torpedo onions stand turgid to the sun and muck melons inch to take over the path.

I get in my Toyota, and realize I abandoned a banana peel in a half-emptied cup of coffee last week. Fecundity stacks the air so thickly that a coin could duplicate itself on the dashboard, and I have to open the windows to let a very slow breeze infiltrate the space before driving away. Over the last twelve hours, I've become obsessed with Gina. I keep going back through the two days since I've met her, isolate every conversation, rethink the various feelings that the Sierras or Appalachians inspire, and echo her sweet southern inflection on the word "Manzanita."

On Interstate 80, Saturday weekend traffic makes the drive a series of stops strategically placed to make me late. I am an aggressive driver who has honed her skills in DC commute traffic, and I speed up to seventy only to stop at ten for a minute before accelerating again, like runner doing intervals on a treadmill. I finally break through the traffic and climb up and down the hills that create American Canyon. Just when it looks like I'll actually be on time to meet my friends, I hear a loud "pop" and suddenly my car swings to the right.

The wheel shakes and it takes all my strength to hold it in position long enough to signal and slow the car toward the highway's shoulder. I'm shaky, but by now I've become seasoned to tire blowouts. When I lived in Oakland this happened at least once a month. I'd be careening over a highway ramp only to feel the familiar pop and shake. My street in Oakland seemed to collect broken beer bottle glass, bizarre metal ends, and smashed windows. If it weren't the tire blowing out on the road, someone would key my car or throw an egg on the hood. I've become very good at changing tires. So good that I couldn't afford a replacement tire or spare the last time this happened.

I wait for the tow truck and watch coastal fog billow in from the bay to nose the red, blue, and yellow roller coaster tracks at Six Flags. When trucks pass me in the right lane, I can feel my small car tilt and lift from the pavement—but I feel potential in every swoosh. When the tow truck comes I jump out and wave my hands, like a little boy vying for a football pass. Now I have an excuse to go back to the farm and see Gina before she flies to Seattle.

August, 2006

Back in Vacaville, I call Janice and explain my situation. They're about to leave for Tahoe, but she says they could swing by the farm and pick me up. It is on the way after all.

"Oh, it's okay. I think this might take awhile. You guys go ahead. Hey! Maybe we could hit the beach next weekend?" I stand outside Big Four and look at my car that's been waiting in the queue for fifteen minutes.

"Yes, of course we could hit the beach! But are you sure, sweetie? You are on our way…" Janice sounds thrown off by my sudden change of heart, and I can hear her zip a duffle bag and inhale a spliff in the silence after she speaks.

"Yeah! Yeah, you guys go ahead. Have a blast! Love you!"

Big Four Tires has free coffee that's a little weak and cold, but I sip the brown water and flip through a book of Jean Valentine poems I've kept in my car for emergencies like this. In an hour they've replaced the tire and hooked me up with a cheap spare. I roll out of the driveway at 2

PM—just enough time to make it back and clean my yurt before Gina and Baker return. I slide past gas stations, thrift stores, and Mexican markets, try to figure how I can seduce Gina into a kiss.

August, 2006

I've washed my week's worth of dishes, swept an inch of dust from the wood floors, stacked my buckets of oatmeal and black beans, and made my bed with clean sheets. All that took about an hour, and now I'm trying to keep my mind off the coming task by flipping through Whitman's Leaves of Grass: I'll read a line and my mind throws up an image of Gina's smile, her smooth flush lips, her tanned forehead.

At four, I can hear the chain slip down to the ground and the gate to our yurt village creak open. I slip out to the tree and pretend to be collecting my laundry when they approach. I explain what happened to my car, and try to emphasize that it's no big deal, I don't sweat the small stuff, I'll just head into the city tomorrow and stay with a friend.

Every inch of me is pounding as I talk. I try to navigate the line between being happy to see them and bummed out about my missing trip. Gina seems happy to see me: she tells me about the dinner they had at Jardiniere; the stuffy waitress that served them, and whether each dish was perfect, slightly bitter, sweet like thick honey, or a little overcooked. We both smile as she turns to walk toward the camper van. She springs over the worn ground in between our dwellings, hopping over old misters lain like bones in tall seeded grasses. My hands shake as I handle my socks, stiff as emery boards.

August, 2006

After a half hour I can hear Baker and Gina talk just outside the camper van. I don't know what to do. I feel trapped in the yurt's canvas and unable to make a move—my taunt stomach churns and feels as if butter will explode out of my sides. I fear I wouldn't know how to make a move if it bit me on the hand and said "Here look: do this, and this, and this."

I'm starting to feel faint and realize I haven't had anything to eat but a PowerBar and some left over spicy black beans. I decide to make quinoa. I cut fresh torpedo onions I culled from the field on my way back to the yurt, and sliver sticky cloves of garlic. In the pot I add onions, garlic, olive oil, and a heaping tablespoon of Pimenton de la Vera. The pimenton dyes the fast moving oil brick red; onions and garlic fill the yurt with a heady aroma, and I imagine I'm in a fish market in San Sebastian overlooking the Atlantic.

After about a half hour, the voices stop, and I hear Baker's boots clear through the grasses on the way to her yurt. Here's my chance, but I don't know what to fucking do. Why do I have to let any chance of love just slip through my fingers? How am I worse than Eichmann? The worst I've done was nothing, and all the love I missed with that first woman I fell for comes back to stick me in the gut like a tetanus shot at the very minute that I add quinoa to the pan.

Then it hits me.

Everyone needs to eat dinner. I could just invite Gina to eat. Maybe she'll say no. Maybe she's not hungry. Maybe she'll want a bite to eat. It can't hurt to ask. I don't have to do anything but offer to feed her. Maybe I can just ask if she's single or something. Casually. Even people that are just friends ask me if I'm single. It doesn't have to mean I want to fuck you all night.

I add water to the quinoa, cover the pot, and turn down the flame. Every step becomes linked to the next, and I no longer feel my body shake as I walk to the camper van. Through the side door I can see her on the bed with her sketchbook. I walk up the creaky steps lined with sandpaper, and lean in to talk.

"Hi Gina."

"Hey Cheffy!" Another big smile, she shifts her legs to face me. The camper van's decorated with floral prints and orange towels Farmer got at Goodwill, and the bedspread's blue delphiniums crinkle near Gina's jeans.

"I'm just making some quinoa over in my yurt, and was wondering if you'd like to come over for a bite to eat?" My voice doesn't sound like a thousand little needles of self-doubt are emptying every vessel in my body of their blood.

"Quinoa? Yeah. Sure, that sounds nice." She sets her sketchbook on the bed, and looks at her watch. "I'm supposed to meet Oliver up in the kitchen, but not until later. So yes! Quinoa would be nice." Gina smiles. My heart sinks down, grabs a hold of my toes, and wrenches up to my stomach.

"Ok! Great. I'll...it should be done in about five minutes. Just come over whenever you're ready."

Between the camper van and my yurt, I see a deer suddenly jolt on its hind legs down into the dry creek; her hoofs scatter loose rock and dirt from the bank. The neighbors are having some kind of pool party, and even four hundred feet away I can hear the cannonball splash

of a kid and the subsequent scream of cold shock and joy.

August, 2006

Gina comes into the yurt, says: "Thanks for the offer," and sits squarely on the edge of my bed. I stir my quinoa, and know that if I don't just do this I will be banished in my mind: I might as well just give up pretending I'm alive and go live in a cabin far away from any scary human contact, where I can write about nothing but the hum of bees, bears eating salmon, and the dramatic turn wind makes through valley passes.

I ask if she's single, she says yes.

I ask if I can kiss her, she says yes.

Next, I feel her close to my side and we're bound by tongue and hand. Skin and pressure that I don't want to stop.

August, 2006

An hour or two later, we get dressed and eat quinoa. We talk, and the idea of holding a conversation now seems more difficult than the seduction. There we were: joined, feeding each other, and now we're as separate as two people just getting to know one another. That sudden distance. I don't really know anything about Gina, and the honest truth is I might never know her as she travels to live her new life up north. A part of me wants her to just go now, stop or suspend these feelings that I'm beginning to have that make the yurt's dense air caustic and confecting all at once.

August, 2006

Later that night she's in the camper van; I'm in the yurt. Coyotes and donkeys scream and call into the vast spaces of pasture. Silence in between their noise. I can't sleep. Too much potential that I'm leaning over, like I'm on a cliff.

August, 2006

Goodbyes. Early morning kiss. Promises to keep in touch, visit. We exchange numbers and email. If I can somehow stay in her life, maybe in five years something can come of us; but the fact that there must be years in between, and we will both have to date others in this between, makes this morning encompass all mornings ahead of me, quiet with cool dew rise.

Before the sun ascends to steal moisture hidden under okra leaves, Gina and Baker trudge through the field on their way to the airport. From the car window, dew expands into mist that steadily fills the space above corn, soy, and strawberry crops. Cars mumble past Baker's old SUV; their noise slips in through the door that doesn't properly close, makes the car fill with motion. Movement converges against the windshield from the road's yellow lines and noise builds itself with each passing car. On her way, eucalyptus fingers comb through the thick air. Manzanita leaves shine as the sun shimmies itself between the mountains of American Canyon. The excitement of what comes next fills each swoosh and wheel tick. Gina will be twenty-nine in five days.

August, 2006

"Trunks heavy, smooth, gray barked, gnarled in really old trees, picturesque in silhouette. Leaves rough, bright green, with three to five lobes, 4-9 inches long and nearly as wide. Casts dense shade... As tree grows, prune lightly each winter, cutting out dead wood, crossing branches that interfere with traffic. Pinch back runaway shoots any season."

-Sunset Western Garden Book

This week we start harvesting figs from the neighbor's monstrous tree. From one main trunk, numerous offshoots sprung to become tall twisted trees. Farmer, Baker, and I each go our own way to hunt for the fruit among the leaves that brush us like hands.

When you harvest figs you must thrust your body into the mess of leaves and branches, work yourself into the canopy. Underneath the limbs you can look up and see numerous figs, which sag like drops of water about to fall from the points where leaves join the tree. But you would never be able to see all these possibilities to pull at if you looked at the tree from the periphery. You have to go into the tangle, and chance that you might only get dried

leaves in your hair and scratches on your face. You might

look up to green under-ripe fruit, or branches that end in

knobs of bark, dry figs on the ground like corpses.

Once you find a patch and pluck thirty perfect figs for

the basket (nine for your mouth), you get brave, willing

to climb the most precarious heights of the tree just to see

how high and risky you can get for the fabled fig. You

see the plump dark drop from ground level, and climb

and shuffle your feet along the knobs of bark to reach it.

You cannot be sure you will be able to grasp the black

sack, but you propel onto narrow branches like a joneser

lights an empty pipe in the hopes of a resin high. Maybe

because your hair gets snagged and you slip and fall

against poking branches, the fruit tastes more intense,

honeyed and soft seeds burst against your tongue.

August, 2006

Beach weekend. Janice, Ricky, and I hit the nude section
of Baker Beach in the early afternoon. The cool ocean-
infused air soothes past our bodies and up over the cliff
lined with perverts taking pictures of nude bathers. I
don't care. I will sit naked and read Sexton's Love Poems,
make the perverts irrelevant in my vision of beach and
sunny day lounging. Janice and Ricky play in the surf
like young lovers: they hold hands and jump over the
small broken waves, then pretend to run from the next
little ripple as it climbs the beach. Janice runs back to
our towel section with a handful of glinting beach glass.
Green, blue, and clear pebbles seem like jewels as she
passes them from one hand to the next.

I want to be on this cool ground all week, my body sore
from climbing fig trees and pulling at odd angles. When
I look up from my book, a squadron of pelicans glides
ten feet above the wave line, searches in the fitful surf for
lunch. One breaks free to fly further from the coast, only
to dive straight down like a javelin determined to pierce a
fish's ample belly. When she rises with a sardine's fatness

in her mouth and seawater sliding into the waves, I want

to steal her catch and pry firm flesh from the fish's thin

bones.

August, 2006

When I get back to the farm, the afternoon's heat bakes driveway gravel into the ground. The air smells like roasted grass.

I drive to the level gravel clear of tools and machinery before the navel orange tree that has become my parking space, and lift my grocery bag stuffed with crackers and food bars. From the corner of my eye, I see Jules' old Subaru stuffed with closed boxes and rolled carpets. The whole upper section of the compound hovers in silence: everything rises, silent from the packing shed to the empty greenhouse to the outdoor kitchen. No sign of Farmer, even her truck's gone from its normal parking place near the hemlock.

August, 2006

Before we start picking tomatoes today, Farmer looks
down at the dusty ground and browning grasses before
the field and says in a low and quick voice that she told
Jules to leave because her drinking has gotten out of
hand. After that, while we concentrate on harvesting all
the ripe Sungolds and Red Cherry tomatoes, Farmer has
her earphones in. Every now and then Baker and I talk
about our weekend excitement, but most of the time we
each go into our own head and stay there for hours at a
time.

After lunch, we harvest figs. I ride in the back of
Farmer's truck as the three of us pop out of the driveway
onto Bucktown Lane for 100 feet and then onto the
neighbor's dirt road, past his bee boxes to the figs.
Today's the hardest fig harvest day so far: we picked
the trees lean at the end of last week, and now we have
to hop higher and higher up the trunk and spread our
weight on less sturdy branches to get any soft fruit.

The day wears on us: the dry sun, the effort of climbing
hard on our stiff tomato picking backs. Farmer seems

exhausted, weary and pissed under the large leaves.

After I've taken care to place each fig tip up and ranked

in flats according to size, I see her go through what I've

just done and rearrange all my work. But she doesn't

explain why, just looks frustrated as she sorts through

my harvest, replacing each fig with another identical fig.

Milky fluid begins to bleed from each fruit's stem.

August, 2006

I call Gina and wish her a happy birthday. We talk
for twenty minutes about her housing search, some
installation art that she's seen, and the trail run I just
took to the top of Mount Vaca. The conversation goes
smoothly until the end, with her awkwardly saying:
"Let's keep in touch."

For three weeks I call once a week, text every few days
with less and less frequency until I no longer receive a
call or text back.

Move on, I tell myself on an afternoon when all sounds
from the seasonal creek have stopped and all picking
conversations fallen into silence under fig leaves. The
sunlight weighs on me and I feel like a tomato with
blossom end rot fermenting in between rows.

Sometimes an experience or idea of what's happened
between two people is only yours to own, and no one
else's.

Tomatoes

Many bloated and soft

left to rot

between the rows.

The golden one I lift

barely fits into my mouth,

all the seeds swim on my tongue,

the juice lost to cracks

in the clay soil.

Nothing can root between the vines,

we pull and destroy

tomatillo and amaranth,

their seeds sterilized

in the cricket snapping heat.

Yesterday coming off the interstate,

hundreds lay smashed

against asphalt, splayed onto thistle.

At night I wake to lift my head,

raise my stomach, help the acidic juice settle in.

In the market a man told me

he felt rich with tomatoes in his kitchen, rich!

California, 2002

"Live or die, but don't poison everything." Ann Sexton

When I got off my shift as a line cook, I downed a thimble
of whiskey and drank three or four beers; in my attic room, I
overlooked Oakland and the city's lights. Give me a cigarette.
Give me a hit. I wanted to numb all the voices in my head. The
voices of Mom's disappointment. The voices of Dad's frustrated
punches. The voices of Tony, the boy I thought I loved who
said he didn't think of me that way. The voices of Kat, the girl
I knew I loved and told her so the night before she hooked up
with her new long-term girlfriend.

I couldn't live into adulthood.

I didn't realize these voices were my own, that I needed to
shed them like an onion shoot pushes away dull paper that used
to protect, but now only steals light.

Each morning for five days, I threw a half-full pack of
American Spirit Lights onto the patio. I took the hose and
turned it on full blast, drowned the damn sticks. Tobacco, torn
paper, filters: all they were made of separated onto my patio.

The dry air gave me a purpose: every morning after killing
my cigarettes, I watered my roommate Harold's numerous pots

of geranium, jade, and bay. My wrists had swaths of burns up to the funny bone from hot sheet trays filled with croissants, tarts, and sticky buns. Like a sixth grade boy displays his skating nicks, I showed my scars to friends over beers at Mad Dog in the Fog.

Marlena, my neighbor's kid, helped me plant the tomatoes and zucchini. At first it was fun: I showed the girl how to dig, water the hole, dig some more, pinch the bottom leaves, lower the root ball into clay. On gardening Mondays, I started drinking early. In the sun, it felt right to have that cool bottle and its condensation in my hand.

As we pulled up nets of crabgrass and threw them in the compost pile, she told me of her mom's brain tumor—it kept coming back, grew, hooked itself in. Marlena liked to pack the soil around transplants, make sure the leggy starts were fixed in the ground. At her birthday party, we ate pozole and her mom spooned ladle after ladle of the thin red soup into blue plastic bowls.

The next morning, I couldn't look at Marlena's little brown fingers: they were serpents, wriggling in the dirt, trying to lift the weeds and tomatoes. The artichoke wouldn't flower that summer, even the earthworms had tumors, curled on the soil surface, unable to burrow.

August, 2006

Farmer tells me I can stay on the farm as an intern
when the official apprenticeship we originally agreed on
ends in November. She says we can arrange it like so:
I'll work helping to clean up the fields of the growing
season's debris and do odd jobs part-time in exchange
for room and whatever veggies or fruits I can scrounge
from the farm. I'll be in graduate school about a half-
hour from the farm, and this will be a cheap way for me
to live. When she suggests this plan, I am taken aback,
because I honestly don't think she likes me: she tolerates
me because she's agreed to have me here, but she would
much prefer a situation where she's alone on the farm,
or just with Baker as the season sputters out the last
Sungolds and Jimmy Nardellos.

August, 2006

Harvest day. Market day. Irrigation morning. The days wear on as the sun dries every leaf and stem, sends every plum knob to expand and fruit, full as a breast. Our conversations dwindle as Farmer now listens to her iPod most days. Baker and I talk about her city roommate's exciting love life. Now Autumn's new girlfriend plans a move to SF; she will leave her husband Slick in Michigan with their dog, and set up camp at Autumn and Baker's until she finds her own place.

At lunchtime, I make sandwiches or stuff boiled eggs and coffee into my mouth as I walk to my car. School begins in less than a month, and I'm waiting to hear back from a professor about an independent study on line breaks. I need two more credits, because I've only been assigned a 25% teaching assistantship position.

I've proposed to study Creeley, Williams, Plath, Rich, and Lorca, but it's been three days and I haven't heard back. All of the classes are four credits and I don't think I can swing anymore than two classes and the TA class, especially combined with working on the farm for room and board. My whole success in this strange new world of graduate school seems to depend on this independent study. Professor McPherson knows line breaks; she understands how to use them without cleverness and employs each pause to create something emotionally resonant on the page. But it has been five days, and every lunch break I leave the farm thinking that today I will hear back.

I eye the fig trees that lean over Bucktown Lane as I cruise past; their topmost branches cast perfect figs out into the blue sky's backdrop. At the bee boxes up the road, men in white suits use a vacuum to harvest honey or collect bees. Above the boxes, a few bees swarm in circles like dust brought up by a tractor's back wheels.

Just as I enter downtown I drive gallop to gallop with a man on horseback. He rides down the street like he's on a trail. He even has a cowboy hat shading his longish brown hair and spurs on his boots. We sit at a stoplight bordered by 7-11 and Mr. Pickles. The defined muscles on his horse stand stiff at the light, impatient with the delay. I wonder if the horse's feet and knees hurt from pounding the asphalt and bearing his weight, and the weight of his rider, down the length of Market Street.

At the Vacaville Bakery, I order an espresso and a cup of coffee, sit down in my dirt and sweat-stained clothes, and enjoy every second of air conditioning. The counter is run by high school kids on summer break, and they never seem sure of how they should handle my double coffee order. One kid just throws the espresso in with my coffee; another kid with a streak of blue hair and black nail polish always asks if I want them separate—I don't care either way, just as long as I get my caffeine quick because I only have about fifteen minutes in the cafe before I have to race back to the farm for our afternoon harvest shift.

No exciting email, just junk mail announcing a formula that can increase my erection and make it last for up to an hour. I sip my coffee and gaze out the window, intent on sitting in the air conditioning as long as I can. From the large window I can see my cowboy and his horse trot through town, near the bronze sculpture of a young boy picking a bronze peach with leaves and stems that flash in the rising noonday heat. The bronze boy has a half-full flat of perfectly round and blemish-free metal peaches organized according to size at his feet. My rider and his horse stop eye to eye with the sculpture, and while I can't see his face, I imagine the cowboy staring into the boy's circular eyes, wondering whose son agreed to pose for this unrealistic portrait. I imagine my cowboy nicking or poking a hole in the fine glossed peach surface, or overturning the symmetry of the flat's sorting. But I can't see his face, and after a minute of stillness his hand and strap rise in the air. The horse's muscles tense and release, tense and release as they make their way over the one-lane bridge that spans a dry creek bed.

August, 2006

When I get back to the farm, Baker's left for the Berkeley Market, and Farmer's not in our usual meeting place near the packing barn. I walk around to the outdoor kitchen to find her, but the place is empty and gravel holds the heat so tight that I feel sharp small rocks climb up my ankles as I walk. I sit on a pallet half-cleared of drying torpedo onions in the barn's open section. Through my work pants, I can feel pebbles of dry soil break against the weight of my ass. I close my eyes to still the coffee and heat buzz thumping in my heart.

I try not to think about Gina not calling me back. I try not to think of her at all, but my caffeinated mind can't help leaping toward what it shouldn't dwell on. On the morning we said goodbye, she woke me up and I crawled across the bed to where she sat in her sweatshirt. We sat close and kissed, just for a moment, while the early morning fog lifted itself outside. But what I can't help going back to, and want to stop at, is the moment of crawling toward her; how she smiled at me as I lifted myself over the rumpled sheets and tossed pillow.

When Farmer enters the barn dark as a cave, she still has her sunglasses on. Her hair presses in on one side, like she's just woken up from a nap. She drags herself close enough to my pallet so we can talk. Lily jumps on my lap and tries to kiss my face, but I push her down and let her lick my hand. For a second I think I smell weed, but drying onions sometimes rot and release a similar skunk-like smell.

If she's high, who cares anyway, I think. At times over the last few weeks she's snapped at me—that wouldn't be a big deal if she held Baker and me to the same standard, but sometimes we'll both stack figs the wrong way; or we'll be careful enough, but the figs will lean over and fall in the flats, and Farmer will look at me and tell me to make sure the stems stack straight up because the milky fluid might seep out, bruise, and dissolve the sides of the other figs. She won't look at or say anything to Baker, and I don't want to play the game of who did what when, which is always pointless.

If she's slipped and smoked a doobie, all the best, I think. Maybe she'll stop picking on my work. Maybe she'll relax and smile more. But for a second I'm jealous. To feel your heartbeat, steady and commanding in the chest. To feel ecstatic breath, clarity peak after a hit. I can't enjoy the high anymore: my lungs collapse and I cough like an emphysema patient; I can't seem to get myself together to speak or follow a conversation for more than one sentence. Immediately, I feel guilty for wishing her ill, selfish for wishing she'd give into her addiction just to make life easier for me.

She says today we can tackle the composting toilet in the yurt village. The toilet has been getting a little stinky, infiltrating my outdoor bathing area with a damp rotten stench. I follow the directions on how much mulch and sawdust to add, turn the drum, and empty the tray, but nothing seems to remedy the smell that gets more intense as the summer continues.

Here's how the composting toilet should work: you do your duty, immediately after that you add shredded mulch, and turn a handle on the toilet's side that rotates the chamber where your poop has landed. After a few turns, your poop—either last week's or this week's—

comes out in a bottom tray along with the mulch. You need to empty the tray, throw the mixture in the bushes, and cover with it with more mulch. But no mulch seems to come out in our tray—only poop, no matter how much I rotate the damn chamber.

Farmer and I work together for the first half hour. As soon as I think about why this is my task—not a "Baker and Cheffy Task"—Farmer points out that Baker always uses the composting toilet next to Jules' yurt. I think it's impossible that she never uses this toilet; how can she go up there when she sleeps down here at least a few days a week? Surely, no matter how few and far between her poops, she must use this composting toilet at least once a week.

Of course, I don't say anything—to say anything would be to admit that I can't handle cleaning the toilet. For some reason, even if she's started disappointing me, I still want to show Farmer I'm a tough and solid worker.

We try turning the handle more than once, unload tray after tray. I can't help but make an unpleasant face when some liquid runs into the drum and the pan swims with twenty or so maggots. I have to lift the pan, careful not to let the waste splash over my feet. Farmer says she doesn't understand why this is gross. But I never said it was gross—it just smells and I don't want it on my sneakers and the natural reaction for me is a grimace.

This is where we differ: I don't love my shit. Once it comes out of me, I want it as far away from me as possible. Maybe I'm not tough enough for this farm thing after all. Maybe I should just go back to the city and the flush toilets that remove me from my own excrement?

Farmer tells me to keep turning the drum and unloading the tray until nothing comes out. She needs to add kelp to the irrigation system and do some work in the upper barn.

In the heat rank with moist shit I work, turning and unloading. After ten minutes I develop a smooth rhythm to move the heavy drum, bend down to pull the tray out, lift it over to the wild plum tree, and immediately cover the mound with a shovelful of soil. Now grasses, leaves dry as skewer picks, and twigs from the valley oak tree all blend to look like the mulch I throw in the toilet. No smells but damp poop rise into my nose. I turn and turn, but after what seems like two hours, the toilet still yields tray after tray of mulchless poop.

No way I've produced all this waste since April. This toilet must have been busted for at least a year. The poop seems endless. There must be a lesson in this: like Siddhartha or a character in a bildungsroman, I must be learning something from this repeated action and proximity to my own waste. Farmer must be doing this to show me something. Turn and empty, rotate the drum, feel the weight of your own poop. Feel the weight of your poop and Baker's poop and the poop of last year's apprentice.

When Farmer comes back, I explain to her that no mulch comes out, no matter how many times I turn and empty the drum. She adds mulch, turns the drum, and she only gets more shit, no mulch. She takes a long stick and jams it into the toilet's mouth, moves it around like she's churning butter in the dark orifice. We drum-turn and a little mulch comes out. She does her stick shimmy dance again, and another little mulch load arrives.

Farmer determines that the toilet must be blocked somewhere. She finds two two-by-fours and we lift the whole toilet so it leans toward the front. She brings the hose over and lets it run into the mouth. She turns her stick.

Nothing.

She keeps turning her stick around the toilet basin. I'm at a loss because nothing happens, and we can be damn sure shitty water will overflow any minute. She tells me to take over the stick dance while she tries something.

"We need to work on this hole," she says and guides me to the opening. She turns the hose off and hunches to the ground looking for something. My stomach burns from hunger and the saturating poop smell. She comes back with a longer thinner stick and takes over. She tells me to go over to the other side and check to see if any water runs out.

"A very small trickle," I shout. Farmer continues to work and pry her stick into the toilet. After a few minutes a stream of brown liquid, slivers of wood, and small mulch sticks come flooding out of the toilet back. All the nasty water runs down to a small indentation before the dry seasonal creek, accumulates until it reaches over the bank and falls against dusty rocks.

We stand under the broad reach of the valley oak: sweaty, stinky, exhausted. I can hear my poopy water, and all the past yurt dweller's poopy water hit dry rocks. Farmer's blue eyes glow with exertion and a momentary yield of frustration. The bones under her eyes sink in fast-forward as night shadows our place underneath the oak's lanky-leaves.

Pleasants Valley

So, fall desiccates the land,

cracks salt crust, leaf, archway

of the woman held in this elevated valley.

Hello to crabgrass by the road

and all she pulled for the eye.

Already too much vision in the world,

too much wind, blowing

poor leached dirt from the valley.

Her brows are low.

Small closed eyes.

She's spent her whole life in the shifting acres.

Her woman's got nothing but a full truck.

Her hunting dog rolls in sharp-grass, pants.

Massachusetts, 1996

*In my dorm room, the sun's fixed at noon. High-pressure
sodium grow lights lower close to the tips of 100 clones from
my mother plant. She's over a year old. I smuggled her from
Massachusetts to Jessie's place in Columbia, Maryland for
the summer. Jessie and Carlos almost killed her, forgetting to
fertilize her and ventilate the closet home. On the six-hour trip
back to college, I held my Toyota to fifty-five miles an hour.
I shook as I paid for my coffee at the 7-11 outside of Trenton.
That night, every approaching car light was a cop car.*

*Now I've got her sticky sweet; her buds smell like a cross
between grapefruit and artificial grape chewing gum. The thin
cuttings reach from their Rockwool base toward the light. Every
morning after I take a few hits, I lift the cuttings to check their
matted growth.*

*This morning the white webs have broken out and attached
to their neighbor's Rockwool cube. I mix Dynagrow in old
two liter Coke bottles, and flood the elevated tray with bluish
nutrient water. This mixture is their food, but how odd the
color turns when it merges with the roots.*

Mischa knocks on my door with two cups of coffee. Gnomie

knocks on my door with a bong. In ten minutes, the room's haze becomes thick around my mother; the fine hairs of her cola catch the smoky ignition of her relatives.

August, 2006

Nothing adds up yet: I tuck in scent fragments, touch shards. Everything builds; nothing destroys. I put Mom's tongue caked in blood in my brain's bag. I put Gina's hand as it cups my head in the bag. Too much whiskey and weed and self-obsessed fear, thrown up in the bag. The nothing and then the pitch I felt as I drove across country alone and couldn't imagine anything beyond Loretta Lynn's Country Diner in Tennessee. Then sand sculptures arched wide over a sagebrush bloom. Then mud pulsed with greenlings at Pierce Point. A match ignites in the bag's throng. Fragments and shards shift themselves as if to assemble.

August, 1996

Bring your lighter to the sticky kernel of weed. *Pull fragrant smoke in, slow and full; let your lungs expand to their edges with a sweet burn. Let the breath go, slow and full, until your lungs empty; feel absence as wholeness. Now your head spins and breath feels like an ecstatic motion toward life. Your breath makes you want to live.*

August, 2006

Up the incline, you only see red dust about to be unsettled by your running shoes. Pull in the dry air, quick and full; let your lungs open to their edges with the burn and need for air. Push air out, quick and complete, until you're emptied; feel absence as a way to fill yourself. Your head spins and each breath becomes an ecstatic cycle. Your breath maintains, holds you.

Virginia: June 1996

Mounting the mists we brush aside butterfly weed, send a dandelion seed's small weight five feet over. We look for a forest clearing among thin packed second-growth birch and ash, and only near where the horse path breaks away can we find a space big enough for our entrance. Mosquitoes bite and we slap; orioles call on fully extended poplar leaves; under the leaf mat and stem accumulation, worms feel our feet press them down. Our task: plant eight adolescent marijuana plants far enough into the forest so no one can find them, but with enough light from a slight thin in the ash and birch population.

Jess holds the flat of leggy greenlings, and I swat spider webs cast between thin trunks. Two minutes of pushing aside stems that scratch and bugs that seem to live to land on and pierce our tan skin. Sweat begins to gather and slide down my back before it soaks into my tank top. The deeper we go into the dense and damp forest, the more crowded everything becomes: humid air holds us against a pine's new growth; the leaf mat rises and forces us to duck under a poplar's broad branch.

When we get a clearing of five feet by six, we stop and catch unmasked air before brushing aside dead leaves and stems and making the way for our trowel. What I want to get to is the how the light feels as it screens through pine needles and thin-veined birch and ash leaves; how that mid-morning light makes me want to stay in that specific place at that specific point in my life, with my sister silent but close enough that we can talk about Mom and Dad and her boyfriend Carlos and our crazy Aunt Anny May. Light that suspends and hold us up as in amber; forces me to see me as I am: 19 and high and just wanting to stop here and get higher until I am fixed in that dark hollow of a pine's burned out bottom, crowded by tunneling worms, leaf litter, flies that bite as if to snap us into life and out of the un-being that never seems to dull me from the fear of being.

September, 2006

My turn for a break at the Berkeley Market. In the horde of shoppers with sagging plastic bags, I become disoriented. Maybe the numerous bodies hemmed in such a small place make me spin. Maybe the farm and space of the open valley have distorted my body's knowledge of crowd movement.

Before working on the farm, I was sure our bodies had an almost intuitive knowledge of how to react to various environments; like pigeons, we're unaffected by the density and scarcity of strangers on streets or fields. But after seeing only two or three people for most of five months, I've lost all sense of this former knowledge.

Suddenly, everyone seems too close.

I can't expand my lungs to get enough oxygen. Everyone walks slowly: the mother with her easy-glide stroller, the lost well-intentioned yuppie, the type-A veggie-loving executive, the hippie boy with sage smudge sticks. So sluggish, and even I feel like I move too slowly for my own mind.

I want to see something hard and concrete—some

gesture from the mother in the easy-glide stroller or Farmer Joe smiling at me; nothing happens except I see Chef Charlie, who used to head the kitchen at a local restaurant. He's the kind of chef you hear stories about— how one Saturday night he was looking around the walk-in for something to give a VIP customer and a whole pan of crab guts fell on his head. Next thing the sous chef saw was Chef Charlie's knife-worn hand throw a half hotel pan full of yellow guts across three floor mats to the dish pit. The line cooks that worked with Chef Charlie had to work two hours off the clock before their "shifts" started just to set up their stations, or they were screwed and missing their mise en place when service began.

But every time I've dealt with him at the market, Chef Charlie has had a euphoric smile on his face, as if he's just run the hundred-yard dash for a plate of white truffles. Stacey thinks Charlie's happy because he can get away from his wife for those quality market hours—they own a new restaurant together and apparently she's difficult and they have to spend 16 hours a day together.

Chef Charlie picks up one of Farmer Joe's purple

summer onions, and runs his thumb from the smooth outer skin to right where the green part begins to divide into three tips. I slow down my walk, set myself behind the smudge-stick carrying hippie, and watch Chef Charlie as he moves from the summer onion to a small Rosa Bianca eggplant. He lifts and lowers the eggplant in his hand to check for weight, places it in the sunlight, and then feels the skin for bumps and pockmarks. I can see a blemish on the right side of the eggplant he's surveying. I know Chef Charlie sees the mark: how can he miss it? But he turns to Farmer Joe, says something to him, and Joe hands him a small box in which he places that blemished eggplant.

September, 2006

At the SFMOMA. Bodies shuffle to look at each painting in the permanent collection. Rivera's large drops of color. Kahlo's haircut. Klee's little pencil-men with pointed hats.

On the next level, Tomatsu's retrospective. What a flood brings to a Kyoto street. Look ground-up at a burst of cherry blossoms, rain-heavy.

The last photograph: a melted watch stopped at 11:02 — atomic bomb. The thin metal hands and the slightly destroyed glass cover. All down to that exact moment. What precedes the moment: irrelevant. We move forward from this time, like a child who just learned he can make himself bleed by sticking a needle in his finger: squeeze.

August, 2006

Mold's measured growth on a fig: purple opens into white foam. Motion spreads over the sunken skin, a sugary fragrance replaced by browning seeds and pink juice. Once a fig's gone bad, you remove it from the flat, or mold will leap to other figs, collapse each fat drop.

September, 2006

Amaranth, lambs quarters, and duck weed send up stalks filled with columns of seeds. Switch-grass and hay tips bleached by the sun, hollow little skeletons knock against my ankles. Today I ran up the hill toward the water tower, slipped between barbed wire to the cow pastures. On the side of gravel road, a group of six men gathered behind a pickup truck, watched as one man separated skin from a large cow hung with chains from a valley oak tree. A clean kill, a swift harvest. Fall approaches. Fall eases itself between the dry earth and the cow whose head leans toward it, his blood mixed with gravel and leaf.

Passing a Plum Orchard

Thistle grows under plum trees —
dry, mowed down by wind.
The bark split, mossy.

We bear this joy, like
wires at the field's edge
lifting and cutting the air.

September, 2006

The harvest days grow longer, and we're out for hours plucking for flat after flat of tomato, fig, or plum. I can't follow Baker and Farmer's relationship—whether they're a couple or not. Everything and everyone has become more separate here: I pull myself away from Farmer and Baker; Farmer pulls away from me; Baker pulls away from Farmer. Maybe we've all just spent too much concentrated time together.

We no longer eat in gluttonous celebration. When we do eat as a group, I make rattlesnake fritters from a snake Farmer shot under the hemlock tree near her home. Silence over the meal, until we agree that it does taste like chicken after all; everything tastes like chicken, except Baker's peach ice cream.

This space, twenty-two acres, becomes too small for me if I pay attention to what happens in their romance—all none of my business. One day I'm sure they'll settle in together when the season ends. Another day I'm sure Baker has ended the relationship, and started dating someone in the city. The next day I'll see them work

side-by-side in the pepper rows, hear them laugh and
see Farmer's smile linger when Baker has swiftly moved
on to harvest tomatillos. Farmer's bought a fully loaded
outdoor wood burning oven for the upper kitchen—she
claims as an investment in the property, but I think she's
bought it seduce Baker to stay on the farm.

None of my business—I don't care what happens to
their relationship, except on the days when Farmer seems
immobilized by the dark seed leafing in her brain, days
when we harvest figs, and she drags her body to her
truck and won't smile or speak much.

Her ability to cope seems dependent on her relationship
with Baker, but only on the surface, almost like an excuse
to be discontent with her life. One afternoon when
Baker has left for Market, I can see Farmer sink toward
the dusty soil under the plum trees, as if she wants to
lower herself to a safe place under all the switch-grass,
softening plums, and bee-hum, away from all the excess
energy that life throws up.

The bloom of her darkness seems inextricably linked to
my own, but I can't figure how. I'm sick of depression,

my own and everyone else's. I don't want to hear about the darkness anymore: I need to throw it up like a drunk throws up whisky—get it away. I try to shut down to Farmer's darkness and indulgent self-pity, but I can't—I see her lift her arms for figs and see the weights she's tied around her arms hang and pull her down. I want to yell at her to just untie them, it's easy to just untie or cut the weights, you don't need them—they don't give you anything and end up ruining all the possibility in front of you.

Hive-Mind

We go to the field,

taste sweet pea flower and the vetch's miniature

trumpet.

All is silent except for us.

The dew exhausts itself in morning sun.

She takes air into her chest

with every pull at delicate petal,

and its movement inside

the chamber must hurt.

Beneath the crops worms writhe in soil, hide from light.

A field mouse rots near a drainage pipe.

If we could think toward the same goal,

she would hear bees

hum against plum blossoms.

September, 2006

Baker's question for the day becomes a game of "what if."

"What if I start an Internet menu service? I'll write and organize menus, and restaurants can just download them and pay me lots of money in exchange for a kick-ass menu?" Baker's hair has grown long with streaks of brown. She's traded her red visor for a tall straw cowgirl hat, so I can't see her eyes until she looks at me, and smiles.

"Okay, Cheffy, your turn... What if...?"

My fingers, sore from the dark green tomato resin that accumulates after picking four flats, work to pull a gargantuan Purple Cherokee from its vine. I'm never good at these games which require a quick-on-your-feet response, so I go back to my dream of three years ago: "What if someday I own a restaurant with a five acre farm right in back? I'll pull up soil-warm onions, clean and roast them, and in less than an hour they'll be on someone's plate! What if I have olive, kiwi, orange, Meyer lemon, and avocado trees on the edge of the property? What if I make my own olive oil! What if I cure my own olives?!"

"Okay, Farmer. What about you?" I look over at Farmer, but can't see her eyes because large sunglasses cover her face and reflect back tomato vines and rows of soil. She pauses, stands up, raises her hands as if to sweep the whole farm in between her resinous hands.

"What if I shut down the farm after this growing season. Turn all of this into a retreat center. We'll have classes on alternative home building, landscaping — maybe cooking as well. We'll have the first class help build these structures I've been reading about made from recycled paper. We'll have guest teachers come and teach whatever they want…" Farmer takes her large sunhat off, and scratches her curls matted with sweat to her head, "And the best part is that I won't have to be a farmer anymore."

Baker and I pause. I've never thought of Farmer not being a farmer, even when she's shared stories of her time at Berkeley's law school and her life in SF before the farm.

Baker tells Farmer that's a great idea, that she could have a herd of sheep to help mow the lawn, and then spit-roast the stragglers when they become useless in the dry season.

We laugh and continue plucking, and I imagine Farmer's retreat center in full swing, with strangers wandering around the orchards as plums begin to drop with sugar. In a flash Farmer is upbeat again, zipping down the rows, picking tomatoes like an all-star basketball player sure of each motion, as if just uttering this "what if" has changed her circumstances, enlarged a once myopic and caustic world into one of potential.

September, 2006

I've begun to play the game of what if with myself while I wait for shut-eye and the subsequent stop-mind of sleep: "What if I am just like my mother? What if no matter what I intend I can't stop doing something that kills me, that takes me into the abyss?"

Springs Songs

She is occupied with fields — their weeds, their seeds.

They know more of what she will become.

From winter an ignition of green develops,

and she holds to the light of late

spring, the season that births her will.

How can she breathe the part of us that dies?

For years it has been her practice to narrow fingers

in soil, feel a beet root through loam grain.

Her work is leaden with early moths;

seedlings shove decay through soil,

leaves curl at her feet.

Awakening to immature fruits,

waiting for the leaf canopy,

her mouth is motionless– in haste for strength.

September, 2006

The next day Farmer comes into the wash barn to meet me after lunch. She has a stack of papers in her hand. She slams each paper down on the wooden table littered with labels and twisty ties, and describes how the process of building houses from recycled paper works. I'm skeptical, especially after the rainy season last year. I don't understand how a house made from paper will last through December. But she's sure—it does work; a machine makes paste out of the paper, and the mixture is as solid as cement. She shows me a diagram on a process that I don't have the patience to follow. I see the winds that come through the valley knock over desiccated paper bricks, strew bits and chunks into tangles of Christmas Lima vines and orange tree leaves, and irrigation puddles milky with paper residue.

"We could have visitors from all over. My friends could come and teach classes. Layney could teach a jewelry making class. Baker, the art of piecrust. Cheffy, you could teach classes on spit-roasting," she stops and looks up at me from her papers, "or whatever you want. You could teach poetry." The whites of her blue eyes redden with her energy; she talks quickly, emphasizing each word, as if there's more at stake here than I can imagine.

September, 2006

I've figured it out: destruction and creation sprout from the same seed. The energy that drives me to run up Mount Vaca or write a poem is the exact same force that seduced me to drink five shots of Jameson in a row, which made me smoke blunt after blunt until I had chronic bronchitis. The motion that made Mom try to kill herself is the same motion that makes me look for reasons to live.

So close. All held together by some sort of incomprehensible balance beam in our minds.

September, 2006

Farmer's on antibiotics for a sinus infection.

"That's why I was feeling so low on energy the last few weeks," she tells me as we walk down to the orchard to harvest plums.

September, 2006

After Mom's attempt, when I'd just moved back to California from Virginia, for a few weeks little white and light blue moths would tangle down the streets of Oakland as I walked to the gym or grocery store. Wings like driven plum blossoms skittered from stop signs to hotel awnings to bunches of oxalis emerging from cracks in the sidewalk. I took them as a sign that here anything could happen: I could walk down a street in September, creatures like petals careening past my ear.

September, 2006

Driving back to Janice and Rickey's place from El Rio, the Sunday afternoon/evening gay dance party, palm tree after palm tree lines Mission, but all the taquerias I pass are closed. I'm dazed and rushed from dancing in a throng of over a hundred women, sipping a Corona, thinking about all the potential people I could end up with, and still comparing each one to Gina. Women with short gel-spiked and bleached hair; women with long flowing black hair, hoop earrings, and tight black dresses; women with camouflage shorts who smoke and stare at other women as they bend down to tie their shoe laces but look away when eye contact commences; women whose eyes widen as they talk politics and bounce to hip hop beats. I dance with a tough woman in a baggy polo shirt, and enjoy how she guides me in each dance turn, holds the sides of my hips with her large hands.

Even La Corninata's neon sits dim against the window. I turn my head to look down the street—all the lights out, my stomach burns from no food and my first beer this month. Before I turn back, I slam into a silver BMW, my front end smashed, a guy's passenger's side dented, and my red light still red.

A young Vietnamese man in his early twenties donning a reflective turquoise shirt gets out of his car and stutters "It's okay," as I apologize profusely. He's fine, only his car door is marked with my car's black paint. If he hadn't seen me, if he'd slowed down, I could have killed him; I could have killed myself.

My front end grinds into the wheel. I can't drive anywhere, so I get the car towed to a repair shop; I spend the night at Janice's calling insurance and rental car companies. On the bunk bed in her spare room, I thank a god that I don't know if I believe in but want to thank, just in case, for keeping me and the guy I hit safe.

September, 2006

The Italian variety of prune plum hangs down like
a drop of glistening syrup for weeks before the skin
turns soft and purple enough for harvest. Finally we're
here; I'm looking up at the fruit strung like Christmas
ornaments to each plum tree. The sun-dried plums were
my favorite product from the farm when I cooked at
Oliveto; like apricots, they have that same kick of acidity
and chew that slowly gives in. Each time I cradle a plum
in my hand, my indentations mark through mold that
dusts the fruit. I eat too many, and after the first hour I'm
filled with fructose and plum water.

In two hours we've plucked as many plums as we can
sell at tomorrow's market. Farmer sends Baker to harvest
the last of the black-eyed peas, while she and I head
to the lower field to harvest more San Marzanos for a
woman who's an avid fan of the farm and runs a cooking
school.

The woman wants at least six flats for a sauce
she's planning, but that variety has slowed down in
production, and several tomatoes have blossom end

rot, so we can only pick five flats. Farmer's energy has
dipped to the point of exhaustion again, and as we pull
the cart filled with flats up the slight incline to the barn,
she says she can't wait for the season to be over.

I know she's not just talking about the tedium of the
work; I know things are dicey between her and Baker,
but all I have is a hunch based on Baker's tone of voice as
she speaks to Farmer.

My reaction to Farmer is optimism. I look at her as we
stride side by side, each pulling one arm of the cart.

"Yeah, the fall will be nice. Cool crisp air. And the citrus
will start bearing!"

Sometimes I'm not even sure I buy my own
enthusiasm. Farmer meets my eyes with her blue eyes
marked red by sun strain. This meeting of our eyes takes
a longtime, and I'm not sure what to make out of it. As if
she expects me to understand something, but I just don't.

"If I make it to fall," she sighs, and again holds my eyes
in an incomprehensible way.

I think she's being indulgent. I don't understand: if
things don't work out with Baker won't she just be in

the same position she was before we all arrived at Tip Top? But then she tells me that Chris' birthday is coming up. Since Chris died, Jules, Farmer, and a group of old friends spend the evening together, celebrating Chris. Only now Jules won't speak to her; several friends side with Jules, and won't speak to Farmer either.

"I just didn't know what else to do," Farmer says as we pass Baker huddled close to the black-eyed pea bushes. Her white shirt seems to absorb sun from the field, concentrate all light and Farmer's gaze.

"What else could you have done?" I insist and look at her, but I can see she's still looking at Baker, so I focus on the aluminum frame of the greenhouse ahead. "It's up to her to sustain herself. No one can sustain anyone else. We each have to take care of our own happiness." As I speak, even though we're talking about Jules, I mean Farmer needs to sustain herself, stop dragging her self around like a sick dog just because things might not work out with Baker. She stops gazing at Baker's back and meets my eyes for a second before focusing on the switch-grass that moves beneath our feet.

September, 2006

It is fall now. Air parches cool, insubstantial. The wind so intense the last twelve-hours, the yurt's canvas billows as if it might to take flight along with plum branches and oak leaves. Today, as we took a break in between harvesting zucchini and tomatoes, we talked about the change.

Farmer mentions that in biodynamics they describe this change as a movement from the outward (summer) to the inward (winter). The energy dives inside the soil, inside the crevices of hard land.

Baker says the change is like Challah bread, all the twisting that you follow to the inside layer, uncoiling. Farmer is an engine trying to slow down from fifth gear to second, unable to do so without pushing the engine into abrupt change and stall out.

We feel this tension, impending movement of sorts. Farmer says that we are all at a crossroads in our lives, in similar places.

Wind is a sign of change, and it sweeps away.

The force so powerful it will remove any lingering

cobwebs and litter from the past, carry those now ancient

thoughts to their resting place.

September, 2006

When I reach the wash barn, Farmer comes out to meet me with an empty bucket, collapsed boxes, and some mesh bags we use to harvest okra. Baker's inside, but turns toward the refrigerator, and I can only see her hair, white shirt, and cowgirl hat. Farmer tells me she and Baker need to talk, would I mind getting started without them?

"Of course not."

I wheel the cart and my harvest equipment to rows of okra that now stand chest level. I try not to think about what's happening between these two women I have become more than friends with—my feelings for them are as complicated as my feelings for my family, maybe even more complicated.

I snap pod after pod off the stalks that have grown thick and wood-like, trying to be as efficient as possible since I'm the only one working, and Baker needs to leave for market no later than 11 AM. Maybe I'm selfish, but I dread working on a farm with two women who have just broken up. I'm afraid that Baker will quit the farm after the breakup, and leave me with Farmer for the rest of the season.

After I've filled two cases with the ridged pods, and my knees begin the dewy okra itch, Farmer and Baker walk down to meet me. Farmer is in front, her over-sized flannel shirt dropping below wrist line. She walks quickly, ready to get on with the day's work, her clear eyes set to evaluate my progress. Baker moves a little slower, swings a bucket in each hand from the wire handle. Lily comes from behind them, performing small leaps until she reaches me and jumps for a hug.

Farmer thanks me for beginning work, asks Baker to harvest basil, and asks me to help her comb through the lemon and Armenian cucumbers. Farmer works from the end of the row, I work from the front. I expect something about her to be different, but she searches through the vines just as methodically as she has on all other days, pitches aside overgrown and bloated cukes, and gathers the nice firm ones in a pocket she makes with her shirt.

When we meet up, Farmer's belly looks pregnant with balls and twists; her hands stained with the dampness that nests under cucumbers. Suddenly, I feel protective of Farmer; I want to talk to her and tell her that all this isn't important—that if she doesn't trip, Baker might change her mind back in a few weeks or a few months—she just needs to step back for awhile, tone it all down a bit.

The truth is that sometimes I feel the same intensity that I imagine Farmer feels; there's no middle ground sometimes—but seeing her from afar like a character is different from being inside and feeling the weight that rises to either crush or lift you.

But what if there is middle ground, and we need to find it?

September, 2006

After Baker and Farmer's morning conversation, we rush through harvesting zucchini, eggplant, and melons, and barely send Baker off to the Berkeley Market by 11 AM. The loaded van kicks up dust that slowly settles on shovels and plum leaves. Farmer and I clean up the wash barn, and set up irrigation for the okra without any major incident. We break for our hour lunch, and I get in my car and speed to Vacaville to get online. The professor has agreed to our independent study, and everything seems set to begin my first semester. I splurge and get a grilled chicken, mozzarella, and pesto sandwich at the Cafe along with my caffeine load. The rosemary focaccia crumbles a little with each bite, but I'm so hungry I pick the crumbs off my shirt and drop them into my mouth.

The café bustles with lunchtime crowds. I sit, watch older couples nibble their roast beef sandwiches and families with young children play hide-and-go-seek through the wooden chairs and table stands. All the smiles, grimaces, and mouths opening wide for bread, meat, lettuce, and cheese make me want to just stay here and watch moments accumulate in the lives of people I will never know.

What compels me? The moments after speech or smiles, when each person looks down after that close contact, and it seems like they're focusing on the chip in their coffee cup or the smear of ketchup against wax paper, but the thing is, they know someone else is right there, they feel that other person—their physical presence. If they want to, they can say something, and twenty years from now, that other person will probably remember when Jim or Sally said xy&z at the Vacaville Bakery and Café. I want to hoard these moments in my mind; I want to hear what they say, and see if I can remember. But my half-hour ends too soon, and I need to meet Farmer in the wash barn in less than 15 minutes.

September, 2006

Farmer's plan: cover the outdoor dining area and
landscaping around her home with carpet remnants, and
then mulch to suppress weeds. Yesterday, she went to
a local carpet store, "Carpeteria," where large loads of
remnants were about to be thrown out. Her pickup sinks
into the gravel with stacks of brown, green, and white
carpet piled on the truck's bed. This afternoon we started
the project that she thinks will take a few days. We heave
and unroll the large segments of carpet near the new
wood-burning oven. Farmer's short in patience today,
and so after she explains the task, she remains silent and
works methodically to get all the carpet down near the
dining area.

After an hour, we're exhausted and the afternoon's light
has started to mellow into overcast clouds. We unroll the
last section for the day, and I look up to five sprightly
moths dance over our heads and toward the after-blooms
of blackberries.

"I love these moths!" I shout to Farmer, as I glance after
the petal-wings driving forward.

She grimaces in distain: "Those are cabbage moths. They spread diseases and make my kale, cabbage, and turnip crop half as productive as it should be. I hate those guys."

The moths pause at the serrated blackberry leaves, before alighting to climb over the fence to Bucktown Lane. I don't know what to do. I just want to remain romantically attached to the world surrounding me on this farm, especially now that the work has started to become routine.

"Let me have my delusions, please," I want to tell Farmer, but she's turned her back and started to close the lip of the truck bed. I feel like a little kid that's just been told that the candy she loves is packed with razor blades and made in a sweat shop that forces kids younger than herself to work for sixteen hours a day without a bite of food.

September, 2006

I have a poem by William Carlos Williams in my back pocket, and I study his lines as we carry load after load of mulch from the tractor to the carpet remnants. I can't figure what or if the poem means anything—the lines should mean something, I think, because Williams gives us a character and dramatic situation. But what interests me are the repetitive and odd word sounds and the images that I don't really connect: "brushwood/bristling by/the rainsluiced wagonroad" and "A cold wind ruffles the water/among the browned weeds"—I imagine a Mid-Atlantic roadside corn farm; how in March the puddles fill slight dips in between rows, wait for spring's humid heat after the interminable winter. I tell Farmer about the "Farmer" poem, and ask her if she wants me to read it aloud. Instead, she takes the paper into her stained hands, and reads silently. The crickets near the scraggily birds of paradise start up in the space of our stillness.

The Farmer

"The farmer in deep thought

is pacing through the rain

among his blank fields, with

hands in his pockets,

in his head

the harvest already planted.

A cold wind ruffles the water

among the browned weeds.

On all sides

the world rolls coldly away:

black orchards

darkened by the March clouds –

leaving room for thought.

Down past the brushwood

bristling by

the rainsluiced wagonroad

looms the artist figure of

the farmer – composing

–antagonist."

－ William Carlos Williams

"That's a great poem," Farmer says, her face brown from mulch dust.

I think about one afternoon when I first arrived on the farm. We harvested fava beans at a rapid pace, pitched our arms into tall leaf walls and swollen pods. I can't remember Farmer's exact words, but she alluded to how people think of farmers as living with nature and being a part of it, but in practice they work to harness, control, and manipulate what nature throws out at us.

Farmer hands the crumpled and soil-marked paper back to me. As she begins to dig the pitchfork into the tractor's belly, for the first time I imagine Williams' farmer as the "composing antagonist," dark and not sure how to function in a world where he can't imagine a harvest in his head or turn the space now covered in browned weeds into towers of corn. He calculates and draft plans that will always miss the mark, but can't stop attempting to compose ordered rows and delineated fields.

Farmer brings herself to the tractor, fills up her fork with mulch. Her weariness seems to grow with each forkful of shredded bark. As two cabbage moths tangle through the tractor's open side and grace the steering wheel, I suddenly feel an immense hopelessness for her, as if she will never be able to achieve what seems to matter the most to her now, unwillingly chained to her role as composing antagonist.

September, 2006

Tonight I get a roasted pork panini and jug of Strauss milk for Farmer while I'm at the supermarket, and drop it off at her house. Above her dining room table hangs the mobile she described this afternoon as we moved mulch and carpet. We were quiet most of the afternoon, breathed in dust as we slid mulch into recycling bins from the back of her pickup truck. She's made the mobile from dried over-ripe okra, huge spikes gathered with twine, stems fastened together to make a wheel, and these other dried pods that curled upon themselves—a milkweed of sorts. I say it's incredible, she could teach farm art as a workshop in the retreat center she's planning.

She asks if I've seen the movie about a guy who makes art in natural places, during low tide at the beach. He watches the sculptures he's spent hours making just wash away. In the rainforest he takes days to form wheels of twig and leaf, only to watch the circles slowly decay. Then she tells me: "What I like about the mobile is that it's temporary: it will decay, leave its form, join the soil."

I think: if Farmer's about the making, the attempt—
not about the permanency, why does it matter so much
if things don't work out with Baker? Is she trying to
convince herself that all this is temporary? I walk to my
yurt and hear the crickets' slowing night calls rise in
pitch against summer's end.

Lament For My Sister At Harvest

After James Wright

Hungry from a touch of rain, water strains

against the rocks in the seasonal creek at daybreak;

I return to the orchard, face the heaviness

of plums, the pull and the weight. By dawn, by dusk,

I have seen her covet solitude,

hold her fingers to a stem.

The pulling up of the body is sufficient

to wound her bones. Those tall branches

take from the turned soil more than minerals;

Fueled by the flame of fall, fruits drop,

lie to rot beside her wicker basket.

The dry season holds her in a bushel of brightness

under October's flight of rain.

September, 2006

Grad school orientation. I'm a carp out of water as I sit with my boxed lunch on the cement edge of a fountain, try to sound intelligent and talk without contractions.

When I get back to the farm, Lily doesn't bark and I go down to the lower field and find Baker alone harvesting Sungolds. She says she told Farmer that she wanted to be friends this morning.

This morning I saw them before I left for Davis, they smiled and Farmer held a watermelon that had seeded in the upper orchard. Baker tells me, as we pluck firm Sungolds, that they split up to harvest okra and plums that morning, and then together harvested zucchini. Farmer said stuff like "I don't see this getting better."

They broke for lunch at 12:30. I arrived back to the farm at 4:30.

After talking to Baker, I start to worry. I ask Baker if I should go get her. We decide that I should call first, she could be anywhere on the farm.

No answer. I leave a message.

Should I go bother her?

Baker says no, if she turned her phone off, she wants to be left alone.

Baker stops at 5, goes to the supermarket, and calls from the burrito shop to see if I want a burrito. I work on the Sungolds until after 6:30, when Baker calls to say she has my super veggie burrito up in the wash barn. I walk through the upper field, but I still haven't heard from Farmer.

Her truck under the willow tree.

I eat my burrito in the outdoor kitchen, and make a quick brine for the ham we traded for yesterday. Torpedo onion, garlic, black peppercorn, parsley, salt, brown sugar—no carrots or celery because we don't grow those veggies here in September.

Farmer's house, dark and silent, leans into the ground. No sign of her or Lily. The oleander lining her back patio sways in a slightly cool breeze as the sun sets and the afterglow loses itself quickly behind the fig trees on Bucktown Lane. Silence wraps itself around her dark house, and flows like black liquid over the herb bed, down the gravel path, onto the broad wooden steps of Jules' yurt, setting a clear path to me in the outdoor

kitchen slicing and chopping.

I'm scared of that silence and how it seems to enter

me naturally, like it has found habitation in my stunned

mouth. If she's done it, she's done it. I can't go there.

Not alone. Not with this silence and darkness covering

everything I see.

September, 2006

When I get back to our yurt village, Baker sits in darkness and blends with rising hay tips. Each step I take over the dried stalks makes the cricket chorus recede before issuing its song louder and louder into the clear night. This is how time stops.

Coyotes wake me with their ruthless shrieks throughout the night. I turn over on my side and think about Farmer, wonder where she is, and fear that she's in her house and has done something stupid.

September, 2006

The morning comes and I am thankful for light, for
the noise of a neighbor's tractor, for the Steller's Jay that
squeaks from the black locust.

Through the field sided by wilting melon vines,
chickpeas which never bore, and the last crop of San
Marzanos, I hope when I get to the wash barn Baker
and Farmer sit on a pallet drinking their coffee, set to
begin another harvest day. I need to keep my mind busy,
need not to think that Farmer won't be there and need
to reserve my rental car for another day, so I'm on the
phone when I get to our normal meeting place in the
barn. Baker eats olive bread torn off the loaf in chunks.
I finish my phone call, and ask her where Farmer is. She
shakes her head, she doesn't know. I ask if she's checked
for Farmer in her house. She says no when I'm praying
she'll say, "Yes, but she's not there."

I tell Baker I'll go check. Everything's loud again;
even by Farmer's front steps lined with fifty pairs of
worn shoes, the birds call, and I can hear a car pass on
Bucktown Lane. The front sliding glass door locked. I

walk down the steps. I see Baker and tell her I can't open the door. As I say that I know Farmer's done something stupid.

Around the back patio, past oleander and stray hay tips that have seeded on the side of her house, the back sliding glass door is locked too. My heart's beats, insistent and loud, begin to crowd out all other noise as I walk to the only other entrance, the swing door that leads to her kitchen.

Open. Dishes stacked and fallen in the sink. Caked egg on her cast iron skillet, parsley, crusts of bread, a dried persimmon. Her table with seed catalogs, books, the mobile hung to her chandelier. A scarf thrown over a chair. Wood floor. Farmer. Lily.

September, 2006

Blood on the floor in a puddle near her curly brown hair. Lily at her feet—stiff little white legs. Both dead. The silence dives in through my eyes and spreads point by point through my gut and lungs, wedges itself in my esophagus.

I run to the kitchen, but turn back, still not convinced of what I've seen. But she's still there, melting into the wood floor. Lily is still on the carpet, her eyes staring straight at Farmer.

September, 2006

The yellow jackets don't mind me because of rabbit flesh near discarded pots. The rabbit's hind is bare of fur; Lily's marks still visible through the jacket. In the bottlebrush tree, hummingbirds plunge at emptying bells, retrace their earlier beak prints.

Baker circles over the gravel path near the motor home's shoe-laden steps. Mint tufts that surround us raise as if to infuse the air with a newness I cannot smell apart from what I've seen. Crickets momentarily pause as I shout at Baker not to go in. I hold Baker's forearms, trembling warm under flannel and cotton. The sheathed insects start their choral work shaded by a bird of paradise.

Farmer's done it. I've found her.

The image is inside me now. Fixed her blood. Fixed her spilled mouth. The cabbage moths extract dinner from loaded leaf heads, and fall like petals on the neighbor's irrigation pipes. The emptying out of everything around me but me makes the cricket chorus stop and then pick up again and not stop.

September, 2006

Baker and I pace in the gravel driveway. I try to keep
an eye on her; she can't go in to see Farmer like that. I call
the cops, and they ask a few questions and send a car.
The only way to go is away; we walk down Bucktown
Lane. The neighbor's fallow field planted in vetch to
our right. A dry creek, burned out blooms of buckeye,
twisted oaks that lean like bent humans toward the road.
I can't keep track of what we say.

Was it Baker who said: "It is scary standing between
someone and the abyss."

Was it me who said: "You can't stand between someone
and the abyss, especially when the abyss is inside them."

A grasshopper snaps and rises above the vetch only to
collapse on a leaf and snap and rise again, without any
reference to the others. I watch Baker, watch her eyes
dark as if they've been pushed deeper into her head. Her
hair wisps wildly behind her hat. I'm mad at Farmer
for throwing herself on top of us, as if we're in a sea,
treading water, and she's leveled her weight over our
heads in an attempt to push us down with her.

Who did she think would find her?

September, 2006

The cops ask us questions:

What is her name?

Who else lives on the farm?

How did you two come to live here?

What relationship did you have with her?

When was the last time you saw her?

When was the last time you talked to her?

Do you know of anyone who wished her harm?

Did you hear any shots?

The coroners do their work. Baker and I wait in the driveway to figure out what next. Humidity sinks the air down upon us as we stand on the gravel rocks. Each breath's movement feels labored in that sudden weight. I turn toward the house that I've been trying not to look at, and watch the coroners move her down the steps in a stretcher. Her curly hair pushed to one side where she's lain for hours. Her hand, the one that held the gun, stiff, grips air. Her thumb points out.

September, 2006

I follow Baker to her place in the city. She drives her
car; I drive mine. I have Farmer's phone, and on the drive
I've set myself the grim task of flipping through Farmer's
phone address book, calling her family and close friends
that I've met or heard her talk about in the fields. After
the third call, right before I enter the Bay Bridge toll
plaza, it feels as if my small car's dashboard caves in.
The rain starts: fat drops hit the windshield as I climb the
bridge's first hill.

At Baker's, Autumn makes us tea and we call Jules.
She keeps saying "What?" over the phone, and won't
believe me when I tell her what happened. I pass the
phone to Baker who tries to tell her again. Jules comes
over immediately. Her eyes bloodshot from crying. Her
blue overalls bright against her bleached white t-shirt.
Her rosy cheeks and her silver-blue eyes. I imagine she
blames herself, just like Farmer's father blames himself,
just like Baker blames herself, just like I blame myself for
what Farmer felt she had to do, for what Farmer did do.

The First Rain of Fall

We leave the tight skins of cherry tomatoes splitting
themselves.

As we hum down 80, the bird song

that sounds like a car alarm plays in my head,

joins the sizzle

of car wheels slapping unctuous pavement.

In rearview: upright

dumbfounded swathes of yellow grasses,

spiked cardoon cartilage begins decay.

When we reach the city,

the bodies I am thankful for

—hands weathered by salt wind

leave the cover of jacket cuffs,

finger bus change

in their open palms.

September, 2006

1:37 AM In Janice's spare room. Farmer's dark blood, how it climbs in the space between the wooden planks. Her mouth open to the floor. Lily's still stare. Air pulled out of me. What scares me: the image has no emotion attached. Like a photo I've just seen at a museum. Only there: only sight without anything else. I should feel horrified or like darkness has shrouded all light, but all I feel is what I saw.

3:52 AM Air pushes out. I can hear Janice's roommate snoring across a narrow hall. On the top bunk bed, my sheets gather against the wall. Sweat pulls down to my backside. Farmer's hair, pressed in by blood. The floral print curtains muting morning light from the living room. The stillness of her mouth: fixed open.

5:34 AM I can't breath until I wake up and inhale. Holding breath in my sleep. I'm not in the yurt—I'm in the city, at Janice's. What happened: play the scene. Lily dead—was she shot, or did Farmer give her pills? I couldn't see any blood on her, just her eyes looking out at Farmer.

6:49 AM Hands curled around. Holding the old Remington like a stuffed animal. Her upper lip pushed out. Her chin dropped low. Flies circle and hit the window, as light pulls into the living room. I can't feel anything. Why can't I feel anything? Feel something.

September, 2006

I went back to the farm today, left the cool fog of the city. Before I left I went inside the motor home to say good-bye to her brother and father. The cleaning crew had just left. They had to cut out part of the hardwood floor where the blood had seeped into stain.

September, 2006

The smell was horrible. I felt sick, felt it all come back, but worse.

When I found her I couldn't smell or hear anything— only vision, only image. The smell of her blood pooled there, soaked since Wednesday night.

October, 2006

"Please think for a moment about the word slow…
Combining ingredients the day before so that their
flavors will blend is 'slow.'"

– Paula Wolfert

Death is messy. When people kill themselves, do they
think it cumbersome to shed the body, move beyond its
form, situate the gun so it does the job, swallow enough
pills to cause oblivion, wait out the time of suffocation
while drowning? All the forethought, all the logistics
must take time. Suicide seems like such a spur of the
moment decision, but once it is decided it must take time,
and that time must be imperishable to the self. How can
you not change your mind back?

For Mom, time was walking up the stairs to the
office, finding the bottle of Ultram, opening the bottle,
swallowing enough pills. Time must have taken so long
to get the pills down her throat, and then she had to get
time together enough to walk back down the stairs, to her
bedroom, to her and Dad's bed.

For Farmer, time was giving Lily the pills, locking the

272

sliding doors in the front and back, loading her gun,

figuring out how to hold the gun and where to shoot, and

then pulling the trigger or cage back.

Effect

When we leave the valley, oaks hold leaves.
Gravel, mossy and dew-wet, presses in mud.

At ridgeline, a gnarled fig tree
breaks coastal wind from the valley.
Each branch, once bitten to nub by cows,
divides and extends a thick web.

She tells me this tree can't bear:
stems twist and knot on themselves,
keep sun away.

Satanic graffiti brightens a beige water tower.
We stand on the bald ridge, watch
her plum tree orchards interrupt woodlands.
The terrier, hungry, eats cow shit flattened and dried in
today's sun.

Frogs rise from networks of flowing creeks,
begin to drum and beat
a choral of consistent peeps.
In our silence,
they confect an incipient spring.

October, 2006

When Farmer showed me how to shoot a rifle with her grandfather's old Remington, she made a target out of beer cans and last year's winter squash. We moved onto pictures of George Bush and Dick Cheney that she printed from some website. She propped red beets behind the pictures, so when we shot, they looked blood splattered.

October, 2006

Two nights after Farmer kills herself, I go to a party.
I meet up with Janice and Ricky at "Community," a
biannual party to benefit our friend Malaki, who became
a quadriplegic after a car accident ten years ago. As we
wait outside in a loose line for the bouncer to let us in, I
lean my back against the brick building in the alley. The
brick's cold grain presses into my back and I look at the
locked gate to a garden across Folsom Street, between the
auto parts dealer and an empty warehouse. The urgency
to move in this space so populated with the evidence
of people hits me; the possibility of something else
happening, while she has ended herself.

Inside we break off: Ricky to talk with the other DJ
setting up, and Janice to the bathroom. I start to move my
feet, shuffle like I am slowly jogging, almost dancing, but
I am just moving to feel a body's relief in the possibility
of movement. The drum and bass kick up, and the dance
floor crowds with people in groups of two or three. I
start to jump up and down and sweat as the bodies move
closer.

I am here, I keep telling myself: I am in a body.

A body.

I have been trying to arrive back in my body these past two years.

Did it take seeing Farmer's body loosened from itself for me to inhabit my own? Or is this just what I tell myself today?

October, 2006

The moon gets larger night after night. Tonight we see craters and white spots through San Francisco city lights. All night Baker and I walk, under this huge light.

As we walk up Market, this feeling comes over me: we will go on, experiences will accumulate and stack, but never culminate. I don't know how to describe the feeling—the same exhilaration you get from an epiphany or a widening of barriers, when you see yourself as a part of multitudinous whole.

The feeling happens after we look up from the sidewalk to see the moon, a giant halo touching a space in the sky before apartment buildings.

The feeling is still with me as we walk up Market, past nightclubs and bars, drunks and homeless men with books laid out in front of garbage bags.

October, 2006

I went back to the farm yesterday for Farmer's memorial service. Scared to go back, I had a block in my mind around the scene. After I walked around, talked to her friends and our customers, and plodded the tomato rows, this solidity settled in. Here, the land she harnessed and shaped for seven years, and suddenly she's gone. The energy of sweat and soreness to make those twenty-two acres bear fruit and leaf stays in the soil and plum trees for at least a little while after, but plants untended for two weeks become unruly; okra stalks tower over our heads, pods harden and bloat, tomatoes split and fall to the ground, ferment between rows, scent the air with overripe sourness.

I don't believe any real part of Farmer lives on in those fields, but she worked her ass off in that place, a manic woman, trying and trying to unearth something inside of herself, trying to make something inside herself perform in a maintainable dance with the tomato and zucchini leaves.

How do you sustain the self, sustain desire to live?

How do you balance or maintain? No matter how hard you dig, even if you dig with a large Kubota tractor or polished steel tongs, you cannot find a single rhythm or answer in fields, clay, words, or the amber browned skin of a chicken breast.

After the service, I walked through the plum orchard with Lynn, the Farmer's step-mom. She saw a shrink in Santa Barbara who looked at Farmer's journals. Now they think she was bipolar. It turns out she ordered Wellbutrin, a popular antidepressant, over the Internet under the guise of a 'stop smoking pill' called Zyban, while she was taking Paxil for social anxiety, and heavy doses of sinus medication. This combo could have led to bipolar rapid cycling, and caused her to have rapid ups and downs, until she was thrown into a depressive episode, and couldn't surface.

October, 2006

The next morning I walk around the city. Janice and
Ricky sleep in, so I write a note and slip it under their
bedroom door. The fog hovers over the peaks up Market
Street; thin threads streak into the blue sky above
Mission. Smells of bacon and fried peppers fill the air as I
pass a food cart.

So many people I must pay attention to, from a florist
who throws nutrient water onto the sidewalk near Bean
Bag Café, to little boys from the Catholic school rushing
into the 'Bi-Rite' corner store.

We move. We're on. As if it never occurs to us to stop.

The sheer number of faces hits me.

Each face is a possibility.

I might never know what stories they hold. I can't
imagine what it's like to be the man walking down
Mission Street with plastic bags weighed down from
iceberg lettuce and russet potatoes; his brown hands
bloated from abrasive detergent and water. I can't
imagine how this woman with low jeans, Converse
sneakers, and long brown hair ahead of me feels holding

the woman next to her; their grip seems tight even though they hold their hands low, the space between them small. I can't imagine what it's like to be the young girl running past Bruno's nightclub, the cold breeze filtering through the fog and over her moist forehead. I can't feel the same as the man sorting through avocados in the mercado's bin, each gentle press yielding into a bumpy peel.

I don't know what this means, but every face, every grimace, every giddy smile, every blank stare I see merges for a second before separating again into its distinct place. That is what I see.

Perception

First the plum trees cut by her chain saw,

oil on her favorite flannel.

She drove at the root packed field,

leaned the tractor toe-down,

wedged and leveraged

her place beneath hundred year trees

See what she's made: all ten rows planted,

fritillary crowns of flowering broccoli

brandish bloated mouths to the Delta breeze.

Pea vines, lambent, spring from the dug earth

like rattle necks set to lure light.

When we stand on the swath's edge,

I see cabbage moths lilt, beat

themselves dinner from outer cabbage sheaths.

She says what I will not see, after she says it:

the moths inject

death as they dine, disease

from the neighbor's kale

swelling in the leaf head's close layers.

October, 2007

My question: What we tell ourselves becomes who we are in the end, becomes our reality, doesn't it? What you remember, the stories you tell yourself about what's happened become what happened.

Suicide Song: How She Drew In

She does not rise between bullet-blown lips.

Out of her mouth

    hung loose on hay-dust floor:

        Gourd swell, a plum's plump lift.

Barred fields bud close to my waist.

  Strips of scarlet peppers, bands of emerald okra

    Treble hard to make a chorus of summer's wane.

      Crickets bleat from ditches.

Fume of tomato twined to pole— hooked.

    Bees, pollen-locked, drift to fruit loads,

      Their bodies winnowed, chaff from grain.

Sunflower towers spike ahead,

A thrush gleans seed beneath frail petals.

April, 2009

Story: My mother drank and took pain pills until she was miserable—nothing could measure up, not even herself. Life seemed set up against her; every screw that would not fit its base became a sign that the world was wrong. Did a bitter root distill one horrible answer to all of her questions?

Now she's making her way to a new self without drink. I've watched her shed the old thinking. When I go back East to visit for a week, we end up going on two to four hour hikes through the dense Virginia forests. We talk as we walk over fallen ash and poplar leaves. She tells me how she's involved with AA, taking a Master Gardening class, and raising a smaller batch of chickens.

She's back to my old mom who can maintain twenty projects at the same time, exhausted and enlivened from all of her activities. She's better off now: she has a close group of three female friends from AA that she can meet at the gym, hike with, or go to a meeting with; people she can call and challenge when she feels they are on the edge of drinking again.

We sit on a weathered poplar log and look out over the reservoir. Dogwood flowers unfold and bend from their button-like centers as flies puncture the still surface of protected water. The silence doesn't last long as commuter airplanes take off from a local airport, and she tells me that every day she planned and prayed to not drink, but couldn't stop. Only she did and has.

April, 2009

Make the self lose itself enough to redefine but not kill itself: sustain. The traps are all around; the traps the mind sets to lure us into old stories of our disappointment and disappointments, old stories that tell us we are incomplete and need something from the outside to fill us up, old stories that cast a fearful scenario of what we might become, old stories that limit us by detailing old character traits, when in reality a new self has emerged to assume and supplant the former self.

Speech Turn

1.

Overturned winter wheat, green clumps thrown up.

Down the gravel road near coastal swamp

—how can the smell of acacia, watercress, and horse tail

mimic fern, birch, and black-eyed Susan?

2.

What if she had tried to speak?

3.

At the De Young sits a painting of a lake in the Sierras.

White icebergs float on the cyan water.

I've sat and looked at the painting with two people:

one friend, one lover.

Where water and ridged slope meet —the line

where they join

> *defined,*

like the painter took a knife toward canvas to make the

difference exact.

4.

When I found her

I was heady

with plums fermenting in the orchard

and yellow-jackets on a rabbit's body

—seeing her there, spilling her

    blood,

—what I thought was her

on the oriental rug.

Field flies knocked

themselves against the glass door.

5.

  What was overturned?

August, 2010

On my way up to Davis, I stop in Vacaville to exchange a shirt Amanda bought at an outlet off 80. I am 35 years old. It's still mid-afternoon, so I decide to head to Cold Canyon for a run, out past Pleasants Valley Road. I have to pass Bucktown Lane to get to Pleasants Valley anyway, so I decide to go past the farm for the first time in close to four years. As I drive through town I am excited, like going to a place where you spent much time in but haven't been back to— in a way you are a different person from the one that sighed as she drove past the quick-stop market or held her breath as she walked under the fig trees crowded near the dry creek and thought of Gina. The old town feeling keeps up with me as I drive near the coffee shop where I would check my email, and the hardware store where Farmer and I stopped for wood.

I almost miss the turn onto Gibson Valley Road because a new building takes up the once parking lot. Past the strawberry field we were sure was gassed with methyl bromide; past the now removed stand of wild fennel that I harvested in constant fear of rattlesnakes; past

291

the subdivisions bordering fields—amaranth stalks and blackberry vines twisting stunted by the August sun.

I will never get my feelings for Farmer or for that summer or for this landscape right. That's the thought that makes me drive slow as I near Mount Vaca. On Bucktown Lane, the corner plum orchard is still trimmed and plowed, each tree set with the drip irrigation that Farmer thought unnecessary and wasteful. The street is the same: the goats and sheep in a tight wire-fenced acre near the corner plum orchard look the same; the grape vines that were knee-high when I left the farm, now cast wisps higher than my hair; along the warped wood of the abandoned barn where kids would make out, smoke pot, and drink, the same vines whose names I don't know climb.

Every house and lawn looks the same, except that two properties and thirty acres are for sale. All the same except when I get to Farmer's old farm, the new farmers have built a gray modern two-story house with red shutters where Farmer, Baker, and I harvested prune plums. Every plum tree is gone, and tall awkward corn stalks send tassels toward sunflowers.

How could they tear out all the plum trees that Farmer slowly and regrettably dug up, and whose fruit she would sell at markets? How could they rip out the plum trees whose glossy limbs I awoke to on my first night on the farm, and whose blossoms bees gathered into a chorus beneath? Those blossoms Farmer fell in love with Baker beneath, under their fruit Farmer retreated away from herself.

I turn around as I near the corner where the farm and the new crop of corn end. They have a cute sign in red and blue acrylic paint proclaiming eggs for sale. They have ripped out Farmer's mobile home, but kept the old barn and packing shed intact. At least the land isn't subdivided, and down through the rows of corn I can see tomato plants bushing out fat with fruit. When I get past the farm, the vacant field filled with pokeweed and thistle, where Baker and I walked right after we found Farmer, ticks in the dry heat.

Then the sadness and weight starts filling me like a flushing toilet. Right here was where Baker talked about the abyss, and at this leggy and desiccated weed everything that was impermanent became thrust into

Farmer's ripped mouth. But the wild fig trees to my left flush with hanging figs, and each broad leaf reveals a drop of flesh.

ACKNOWLEDGMENTS

I would like to thank the following people for their influence on the development of *Hive-Mind*:

Baker, I could not have picked a better person work on the farm with. Our continued friendship has made me appreciate you more every year. Keep on baking!

Without Marilyn Abildskov's guidance, *Hive-Mind* would be in my head and not on the page.

Pam Houston offered a place to stay when I had to leave the farm, unending support as I began my writing journey, and lucid stories to guide my path.

Sandra McPherson mentored me in several independent studies in which the farm poems began to form. Her constant feedback, poetry recommendations, and tight poetic lines enabled me to immerse myself in what is poetically possible.

Joe Wenderoth's honest critiques and class discussions on Paul Celan, Hank Williams, Grossman's *The Sighted Singer*, and Williams' *Spring and All* impacted the poetry, and, many years later, the prose in *Hive-Mind*.

Brenda Hillman's mentorship and writing encourages

me to push myself beyond what feels easy and try out different forms in order to press on what can be communicated through the poetic space. Her precise attention to the environment inspired me to reimagine how I present the farm's landscape. Brenda's political activism teaches us that we need to take active stands behind what we believe.

Graham Foust's craft workshops guided my approach to poetry, and his books *Necessary Stranger* and *As In Every Deafness* taught the value of brevity.

I used Wesley Gibson's *You are Here* as a model as I was writing *Hive-Mind*, and he advised me in my early years as an English instructor.

Rusty Morrison provided invaluable feedback on the poems in Hive-Mind.

Rhoda Trooboff, my high school English teacher, made me realize that stories and poems can change people. Her lessons have held for over 23 years.

Chef Paul Canales came into my life at a critical point and helped me adopt productive habits that allowed me to develop as a chef, person, and teacher. He is also the best chef I've ever known.

How can I thank my sister, Jessica, my best friend since I was born? Before I could read, as I battled dyslexia, she would read poetry and stories to me. When I learned to sound out words on paper, we would take turns reading *The Wizard Children of Finn*. Without Jessica's dramatic performances of T.S. Eliot, Ralf Ellison, E.E. Cummings, William Faulker, and Virginia Woolf, I most likely would never have tried to write. Without her care, who knows how lost I'd be.

My brother-in-law, Rod, the brother I never had, candidly convinces me to see events from a different perspective, year after year.

Sara Sgarlat, my aunt and friend, believed in *Hive-Mind* when I was about to give up. She has always cared for me as a daughter, and I am lucky to have her as my aunt.

Lisa Hagan's support and determination to make a *Hive-Mind* a book has been electrifying.

Thank you to the team whose vision brought the book together: Kimberley, Katherine, and Beth. Without your creative insights, *Hive-Mind* would just be a document.

Amanda, thank you for putting up with me as I worked between four to eight part-time and on-call jobs.

ABOUT THE AUTHOR

Gabrielle is an English teacher, writer, and chef living in the Sacramento Valley of California.

For over a decade, she worked as a cook and chef for Bay Area restaurants and catering companies.

During the growing season of 2006, she apprenticed under Laura Trent, farmer and owner of Tip Top Produce, an organic farm that specialized in supplying Bay Area farmers' markets and fine-dining restaurants with heirloom vegetables.

An Associate Professor of English at San Joaquin Delta College, Gabrielle went to graduate school in her early thirties to earn an M.A. in English from the University of California at Davis and an M.F.A. in Creative Writing from Saint Mary's College of California.

Her poems and essays have been published in professional journals and literary magazines. She coauthored a nutrition book, *The New Prostate Cancer Nutrition Book*.

Access link to her poems, essays, and recipe blog through her website: www.gabriellemyers.com.

Access link to facebook:

http://www.facebook.com/authorgabriellemyers

email: gabriellemyersauthor@gmail.com

Twitter: http://twitter.com/gabriellemyers0 (that's a zero at end)

Made in the USA
Charleston, SC
27 December 2015